Burnt

Surviving Against all the Odds –
Beaten, Burnt and Left for Dead
One Man's Inspiring Story of His
Survival After Losing His Legs

Ian Colquhoun

First edition
Published in Great Britain
By Mirage Publishing 2007

Text Copyright © Ian Colquhoun 2007

First published in paperback 2007

A CIP catalogue record for this book
Is available from the British Library.

ISBN: 978-1-90257-828-6

Mirage Publishing
PO Box 161
Gateshead
NE8 4WW
Great Britain

Printed and bound in Great Britain by

Forward Press
Remus House, Coltsfoot Drive, Woodston, Peterborough, PE2 9JX

Cover © Mirage Publishing
Design by Artistic Director Sharon Anderson

Papers used in the production of this book are recycled,
thus reducing environmental depletion.

For my Granny and Grandad, Frank and Edith Merilees. R.I.P.

Contents

Chapter 1
Background

I was born on 7 April 1978 to my parents, Elizabeth and John Colquhoun. I have a big sister named Angela who is five years older than me. I grew up in Craigshill, a district of Livingston in Scotland, a new town built in the 1960s to provide housing and opportunities for the overspill population from Glasgow and Edinburgh. It's a reasonably nice place, lots of nice green areas for kids to play. At first we lived in Clyde Drive in Craigshill, but when I was five we moved up to Elm Grove, about half a mile away.

I suppose I was just a normal laddie. I loved playing football, playing with toy soldiers, computer games and playing 'chap door run', a street game I'm sure we've all played and whose title is self-explanatory. I was quite skinny with really long spindly legs and was asthmatic as a child, meaning that I couldn't run far. This didn't stop me from being goalkeeper for my primary school team and being rather good at it. We were pretty useless as a team though, the low point being a seven-one thrashing by local rivals Riverside.

I kind of had a head start over a lot of kids in my class as my mum taught me to read and write long before I went to school, as well as teaching me a little bit of French, though that was mostly used to wind up my teachers. The downside to being a little 'cleverer' for want of a better word is that at school it's not cool or trendy to be clever. I now know of course that kids who call clever kids 'swats' are actually jealous, but to be honest the people in my primary school class were a great bunch. However, so as not to be seen as 'uncool' I soon learned to use my intelligence to wind up the teachers and make them look stupid, which made me somewhat popular with my classmates, even if it did lead to a few stern rows after parents' evenings.

I was allowed to watch comedy like *Blackadder* when I was eight and I can still see the bemused expression on some teachers' faces when I'd make a smartass comment about the lesson that only the teacher and I understood. This usually led to me being sent out of class, but looking back I know the teachers would have been laughing inside at my audacity. My sense of humour was to forever get me into trouble.

So life trundled on, arguing with my big sister, playing football and generally being a normal laddie. I've been a Hibs fan as long as I can remember and that is something I inherited from my Hibby dad. Apparently, when I was aged five, I came in from playing with the boy next door, who supported Rangers, shouting 'football rangers', as I knew nothing about football at the time. As soon as my dad heard this I was taken to see Hibs and have been addicted ever since. Thank God!

In primary four I appeared as the featured child in a book commemorating twenty-five years of Livingston, the two-page item consisting of pictures of me and my family and some silly drawings I had done. I also played the lead role of Joseph in our school's version of the Andrew Lloyd Webber musical 'Joseph and the Amazing Technicolor Dream Coat', which I really enjoyed. Playing this part gave me great self-confidence and also showed that I had a talent for singing and performing, which I previously had not been aware of.

I went to high school when I was twelve and it was good at first, I even made the school team as a left-winger (I was right footed), which showed how much my asthma had cleared up. Again, I had really good friends. My pals in the street were Graeme and Mark, while I also had good friends in Simon, Dingy, Two Brians, Martin and Andrew.

High school seemed easy enough and there was ample opportunity to play pranks, the pick of which was throwing a pile of geography books out of a third floor window when the teacher wasn't looking, only to have them brought back into the classroom five minutes later by an irate janitor whom they had hit. My friends and I also had a fondness for setting the school skip on fire, which caused much hilarity. Ironically, we had done this on twelve consecutive days without being caught when, on the thirteenth day, someone else set it on fire and I was blamed. My mum asked me if I had done it, to which I truthfully replied 'no' and she went up to the school and got it all sorted out. I even got an apology from the teacher who had accused me, which was ironic considering I had already done it on the twelve previous occasions. I didn't feel very mentally challenged at school and this is why I participated in pranks. At the back of my mind I wanted to be a journalist when I grew up since I didn't seem to be getting any better at goalkeeping.

Away from school, football and practical jokes, I enjoyed going to my local youth theatre group where I met a lot of people, had a lot of fun and snogged some gorgeous girls. Life was toddling along nicely. Then came a bombshell that was to change my life forever.

When I was thirteen, my parents split up and my dad left home. I was utterly devastated by this and, although I saw him a few times after he left, my little boy's brain just couldn't handle the situation. One minute you're coming home to your family, next it's the stereotypical weekend bowling trip with Dad. I just couldn't handle it. My mum always encouraged me to see my dad, even to the point of sometimes harassing me to go, but I just couldn't. It didn't feel right having to meet him like a stranger. After I hadn't seen him for a while he came to our house one Sunday and begged to see me, but I still couldn't handle it.

Whenever anyone mentioned my dad it felt like a knife twisting in my heart and, other than confiding in two or three close friends, I avoided the subject for the best part of the next ten years, building a psychological wall around myself. People started assuming that I didn't have a dad or that he had died and that didn't bother me, just as long as they didn't fucking ask me about it. Anything but ask me about it. The last straw was when both of them asked me about some crap to do with a visa card, I felt like piggy in the middle. What was this to do with me? I just wanted my family back.

With retrospect, my decision not see my dad was the wrong one, as I did of course miss him badly and although my mum had done an impeccable job of bringing me up on her own, she could maybe have done with the wee break. I was also at that 'turning into a man age' where I really needed him. It later transpired that my dad had another woman on the go and this caused a world of shit. Someone threatened to involve the police in their credit card dispute and that was it as far as I was concerned. No one threatens my mum and gets away with it. Seeing my mum so hurt and having a strange empty feeling inside all the time helped me push my dad out of my mind. I even had some wee arsehole in school come up to me and laugh about the fact that my dad had a new woman, and my response was to plaster his nose across his face in front of everyone, and no one EVER came near me like that at school again.

Looking back as an adult now, I know how life can be and that what happened to me has happened to a million other kids and a million other couples. That didn't make it any less painful for me though, and I can only imagine how my sister Angela, who was studying in Northumbria at the time, felt about it all. I didn't have a problem avoiding the subject as a young teen as I was a big lad by then and generally if I didn't want to discuss anything then I didn't have to. I should, however, have done something about it, as this 'shit' (I can think of no better way to describe it) was ultimately to have a negative effect on my life.

I left school at the start of the fifth year and went further into my own shell by not doing much. All I seemed to want to do was play computer games or take the piss out of people via my CB radio. Uncle Ronald, my mum's brother, was brilliant towards me. He took me to Hibs games after my folks split and always gave me a smile and some money, as did my wonderful grandparents, Frank and Edith Merilees. By the time I was seventeen I was attending games with fellow Hibs fans from Livingston and was getting to think I was quite the big man at games. We all went on the East Terrace and later the East Stand when it was seated and we sang our hearts out watching Hibs teams of varying degrees of competence.

The games I'll always remember were firstly the 1993 League Cup Final against Rangers at Celtic park (we lost 2-1 thanks to a late overhead kick from Ally McCoist) not for the game, but for the sight of nearly every Hibs fan (about twenty thousand of us) staying at the final whistle, holding scarves aloft and singing 'You'll never walk alone', despite the fact the Huns had beaten us. The other one was on my seventeenth birthday, a 0-0 semi-final draw with Celtic at Ibrox in which our keeper, Jim Leighton, saved a penalty. It looked fantastic to see the home of Rangers absolutely covered in green and white, and though we lost the replay 3-1 I thoroughly enjoyed the atmosphere. We might have won the cup that season as our opponents in the final would have been crappy Airdrieonians, but knowing Hibs we'd have knocked out Celtic then lost to Airdrie anyway.

Chapter 2
Work And Stuff

In June 1995 I got myself a job with BFD, a local chilled food distributor, as a warehouse operative. The cash wasn't great but it gave my life much needed structure as well as enabling me to go out every week. In some ways this was a mixed blessing, as by then I was a bit too fond of the Buckfast and drink in general: in fact I'd say that's when my problem started.

With the job, however, came a better social life and it did make me grow up a bit, as well as allowing me to make some good friends in the process. I still went to Easter Road every other week and got wrecked, but now I was going to pubs and clubs too. It was great. I even got myself a part-time job in another local warehouse in the evenings, which meant I had lots more money to spend on alcohol and clothes. The work was easy, in fact a trained baboon could do it, so this is perhaps why I drank so much as I was mentally unchallenged.

By summer 1997 I had decided to leave BFD and go full time at Christian Salvesen, the place where I worked part time in the evenings. I had a lot of friends at BFD and it was a tough decision to make, but in the end I opted for the better wages and prospects offered by Salvesen's rather than the friendly but dead end BFD.

My friends at the time, Alan, Darren and Paul, were a good laugh to go out with at the weekends. We had some great laughs but none of them ever wanted to go out anywhere other than in Livingston, which was tedious. At my new job I got talking to a guy about my age called Eric, who by coincidence also knew my mate Paul. We worked in the same department and arranged a night out. It was a brilliant night, Eric and I were good at pulling women and I also got to meet Davie, Eric's ginger haired mate. He seemed like a dodgy character at first but I quickly got to like him and Eric. I started going out with them to Edinburgh nearly every week, with Davie's girlfriend Jenny sometimes in tow. I knew Jenny from school in Craigshill anyway. We had lots of wicked nights out in Edinburgh and I went to work at Salvesen's, which included Sunday work, with many a crushing hangover. The job was going well though and I was promoted to a checker, not much different, just slightly better pay.

The first six months of 1998 were eventful to say the least. Firstly, it became clear that Hibs were going to be relegated to Division One, though the late appointment of Alex Mcleish as manager almost avoided this. I like to think I played my own part in our struggle to stay up, by threatening Hearts player Jose Quitongo a few days before the 97-98 New Year's game when I met him in a Livingston nightclub. It must have worked as he never scored in the derby that ended: Hearts 2–2 Hibs, coming from two goals down with strikes from Pat Mcginlay and Andy Walker.

Early that January came a rainy Friday night when I went out with Davie, Eric and Jenny to Room at the Top in Bathgate, Scotland's best club around for miles. This was to be the start of a three year period of going to this one nightclub nearly every week, initially because the music was good and we knew lots of people there, then later because we were regulars and could get away with doing ANYTHING in the place.

Going clubbing every week, with all the alcohol, dancing, soft drugs and staying up all night, soon took their toll on my appearance and my already weakened mental state, but I rarely let the mental side show. To be honest, when we all went clubbing in 1998 the only problem I had was the party finishing and going back to my mum's to try and sleep.

In summer 1998 my mate Eric was offered a flat in Craigshill and asked if I wanted to share so we could have parties and see different women all the time. The playboy lifestyle indeed. It sounded great and I was glad to spread my wings and move out on my own, after all I was earning more than enough. One problem. I had just started seeing a lovely girl called Marjorie, and Eric had pulled Michelle, a girl he had fancied for ages. It was actually Marjorie who helped me move my stuff with her little Ford Ka, as I didn't drive at the time. That relationship, like most of my relationships with women up until then, lasted only a week or two but Eric and Michelle lasted longer, Michelle moving in with us.

We had some really good times and parties in that flat in Linden Grove, and to be honest things were getting out of hand. The weekends were taking their toll on me and it was starting to affect my work as I often ended up being late. There was also the issue that the flat we were staying in was supposed to be someone else's. The person allocated the flat didn't need it anymore, but instead of giving it up, decided to rent it out to us instead. One problem. The flat holder was receiving housing benefit and we were paying him rent, so technically our 'landlord' was committing benefit fraud. We got away with this for a few months but the council's untimely decision to install new doors and windows in all the flats made things tricky for us.

Eric and Michelle split up, which got a little messy as such things always do, and then we received an eviction notice from the council stating that we were to be out of the house by 14 November 1998. We had been there barely five months but had been rumbled over our landlord's scam, though the multitude of complaints from neighbours about noise and constant comings and goings was no doubt a factor in our being kicked out. We had some good times in that flat and one of the high points was getting to know Eric's wee girl Natalie, who stayed with us at weekends. She would only have been four or five but she was an adorable child whom I got on well with.

Just before we got the eviction notice I had started seeing a girl called Claire, a friend of my wee cousin Emma, who was the same age as me. She was an attractive busty brunette and was a good laugh, and the physical side of our relationship was good, though our contrasting working hours meant that we could only see each other at weekends.

All this time the hard partying had been escalating. I had to decide what to do. I didn't want to move back in with my mum as I saw it as a step back and was now used to doing my own thing, but I was quite low on the council list for a house so that avenue appeared closed. I decided I was going to buy a house, as I was earning enough to do so. But that didn't solve my short-term problem. Eric had moved in with his brother in a flat down the road, a flat which his brother shared with his friend, Martin O'Donnell, who was also the younger brother of my other mate Paul O'Donnell. Three of them in a two bedroom flat seemed a tight squeeze.

I had only just started to get to know Martin properly in those few months prior to being evicted. He was a very funny, very intelligent man, a year younger than me. He also shared the same love for alcohol as me. To be honest, I much preferred hanging about with Martin than his brother, Paul. That doesn't mean I didn't like Paul, but Paul and I were into different scenes now. Martin and Alec, Eric's brother, said I could stay with them when the eviction time came until I got sorted and I greatly appreciated the offer, especially as they didn't want any rent. Davie, Jenny, Claire and I had one last big night out at Room at the Top to see Paul van Dyk, then one last party back at the flat before a work colleague of mine helped move my stuff down to Martin's house. I was to sleep on the sofa. It was one of the worst decisions of my life moving in there, though I was grateful.

Martin and Alec were dole punters who didn't work so they often stayed up late watching tedious shows on cable, which was annoying for me as I had to try and sleep for work the next day. Thankfully I was able to get through it and I stayed with Claire a few times to get away from it all. Martin and Alex's flat was absolutely disgusting. They never cleaned it and the kitchen was utterly ghastly with a smell that I will never forget. The combination of the filthy squalid conditions in the flat and a drunken Martin making stupid noises all night was enough to make me move back into my mum's house until I got sorted.

It was nice to be back, and my mum was pleased to have me back. I still went down to Martin's flat for a drink with them when I moved back to my mum's, we shared a comical fascination with cheap drink and drank many a bottle of Sherwood fortified wine, Country Manor and a bottled beer that was only £3.99 for 20 bottles, all from the local Kwik Save. Eric, who stayed on in that flat with them a little longer than me, must have been annoyed at me bringing drink down and getting Martin drunk then going home to my mum's for some peace, while he was left with all the stupid noises all night. I didn't do this deliberately, but looking back it must have driven Eric mad, though it is also funny in retrospect.

All this time I was trying to juggle work with house hunting, which was very stressful. My bosses were getting pissed off at all the time off I needed, but they understood my situation and as I was one of 'the better ones' I got away with it. I then tried an audacious method of getting a house. I knew that homeless people who worked generally didn't get high priority so I went to my local housing office, deliberately not shaving, wearing smelly clothes and generally looking awful. In perhaps the biggest blag of all time I convinced them I was genuinely homeless. At first they tried to fob me off with B&Bs and horrid emergency housing in Blackburn, a ghastly town near Livingston, but I was having none of it. I went into a rant about how junkies and single mothers and people on the dole could get a house but because I worked for a living they couldn't help me. I didn't actually agree with what I was saying to them but it was necessary to make my case seem valid. I even managed some fake tears. It bloody worked too! Within two weeks I got a council flat in my indigenous area of Craigshill and Eric agreed to move back in so my bills were halved and he could get out of his mum's, where he had retreated to to escape the squalor in Martin and Alex's place.

I moved into 43 Shiel Walk just before Christmas 1998, and there I stayed for the next three-and-a-half years. Christmas that year was fun and ended up with me, Tony, Davie, Andy, Martin and co partying all day in Martin's house after a surreal night out the night before. I was still seeing Claire and I still remember the first night she stayed with me at the new flat. My sofa hadn't arrived yet; all I had was my bed. We had a Chinese meal on my bare living room floor then fooled around in bed all night.

January brought more good news: I had got a new job within my workplace working Sunday to Thursday, 6pm till 2am meaning that the money was fantastic, at least for a relatively unskilled young man like me. This gave me enough money to cover my small amount of bank debt (I owed about £1,700) and to kit out my house. The downside was I rarely saw anyone during the week, as on the Friday I would be partying and then I'd see Claire on the weekend. I only really saw Eric, my flatmate, at work as he worked opposite shifts, which suited us both.

Claire and I eventually fizzled out round about the time I started having parties at Martin's house every weekend rather than going out. My decision to stay in rather than go clubbing was to have very interesting consequences.

Chapter 3
New Friends

One Friday in March 1999 two girls came up to Martin's flat to party with us. Their names were Hollie and Maria. They were a couple of years younger than us, but they seemed up for a good party. Hollie was a slim, attractive Jodie Foster type, while Maria was a stunning brunette with curves in all the right places. Martin and Hollie were soon seeing each other and getting on fantastically well, whilst I quickly started to really like Maria, and we saw each other most weekends. We were like the four musketeers after a while, staying up long into the nights drinking and generally having a laugh. Hollie and Maria soon came clubbing with myself, Martin, Davie, Tony, Jenny and the lads every week, having parties and adventures that make 'human traffic' look like a pensioners' tea party, and that would fill a separate book.

Things went to a kind of pattern. We'd meet up at mine or Martin's house, drink Buckfast wine whilst getting ready to blaring music, then get a taxi through to Bathgate and Room at the Top, the nightclub where anything went. We'd get back from there after a night of drinking, dancing and general mayhem, then head back to either Davie's or Martin's house. Eric was seeing a girl from Edinburgh and still had his wee lassie staying at the flat with him some weekends, so my house was avoided if possible to give him and his daughter peace. Eric moved out to live with the girl in Edinburgh eventually, meaning that we could all start going back to my flat.

Foolishly, one Sunday whilst hungover and having spent my two weeks holiday pay in three days, I got myself a three-and-a-half thousand pound bank loan with which I intended to do up my flat. Of this money I spent a hundred pounds on a sofa and two hundred on a big hi-fi system. The rest was used over the summer for designer clothes, CD's, days out at the football, to subsidise unpaid absences from work and, of course, on partying. The fact I had a three-month repayment holiday before I had to start making payments was a bonus.

And so the summer went on. Work, sleep, watch a bit of telly and maybe go food-shopping midweek, then an enormous party binge all weekend. As the summer wore on I fell more and more in love with Maria, as well as getting on really well with Martin's bird Hollie, and having a superb time clubbing with the lads. However, in the back of my mind I knew that Maria and Hollie were going away to Dundee to go to university that September and I was going to miss them terribly. We had all promised to stay in touch but I had doubts, I thought Maria might meet someone more interesting than a warehouse lad who got wasted all the time like me.

Nevertheless the summer of 1999 was a fantastic one, we all had such a great time. July came and my beloved Hibs were back in the Scottish Premier League following their relegation in 97/98 and having won Division One the previous season with record points. Big Al and I attended a pre season friendly at Easter Road against Middlesbrough with the sole intent of shouting abuse at ex Rangers and England 'star' Paul Gascoigne. I've never really liked friendly matches other than for this purpose, and he certainly got it tight from us. Next week was the big opener, our first game back in the SPL against Motherwell at Easter Road.

The atmosphere as our team took the field was immense. Martin and I joined in with the booming chorus of 'Hibees are back, Hibees are back hello, hello'. In the end the game finished 2-2 with Motherwell equalising late on, but we still had a fantastic time. On the way home to Livingston, two girls shouted Martin over in St Andrew's Square Bus Station. One of them was a very pretty young brunette girl, the other a younger looking gal whom I didn't really notice. It turned out the brunette girl was Martin's sister, Shelley. I was in a hurry to get home so just jumped on the bus grunting an 'awrite' to the two girls, while Martin had a brief conversation with them. I didn't think anything else of that meeting at the time.

A few weeks later Martin and I had arranged to go clubbing with Davie, Tony, Jenny (Davie's girlfriend who was now pregnant) and, of course, Hollie and Maria. Martin and I had become really great friends that year and shared the same moronic sense of humour. He phoned me up that Friday and asked me to go round, but I was going up anyway to see if he was still going out. Martin greeted me as I walked into his flat, by now a lot cleaner as his older brother Paul had moved in to replace the now departed Alex. Martin wasn't alone. His sister was there and she looked totally different to the first time I had met her in that bus station.

No one has ever looked at me the way Shelley did when I walked into Martin's living room, she almost made my heart melt. I knew I was looking right back at her in exactly the same way. I didn't believe in love at first sight until that Friday, though technically it was at second sight, but that mattered little. Conscious that Martin might notice the atmosphere, I started behaving normally and having a laugh with Martin, making arrangements for later that evening. Martin asked if Shelley could come clubbing with us and I of course agreed, though my conscience was a tad troubled as I was seeing Maria and shouldn't be fancying anyone else.

Martin, Darren, Shelley and I were supposed to be meeting Hollie and Maria at Maria's house before meeting Davie and the rest of our crew in Bathgate prior to another gargantuan weekend binge. When we got to Maria's they had already left, but Maria's mum put some make up on Shelley while Martin and I ranted on to Maria's mum about the virtues of Buckfast. The wine had temporarily made me forget about my feelings for Shelley and I was more interested in getting to Bathgate to meet my mates and Maria.

Shelley and I somehow kissed briefly on the way into the club and that was it. I was smitten. I cursed fate for letting me fall in love with two such amazing women at the same time, but when I saw Maria we kissed and we all had a fantastic night together, even pregnant Jenny who was not allowed alcohol and was absolutely rat arsed. I felt high and was having a fantastic time but at the same time my head was in a right mess after kissing Shelley. I found myself taking her hand in the club when no one was looking, I simply couldn't help it.

The rest of the night passed without incident and we all went back for the traditional after party. Somehow it ended up with me, Martin and Shelley drinking cans of Skol lager in my flat, just the three of us, before heading over to Martin's flat again to finish the beer. It had been a surreal weekend and I would never be the same after it.

Chapter 4
Drink

As I mentioned before, I had a bit of an alcohol problem from about the age of seventeen. I didn't start using soft drugs until I was nineteen, but 1999 was the year we all went a bit overboard. Two-day binges every week took their toll on me and I'm sure on my friends too, and getting through Monday to Friday became a struggle to a certain extent. Only the weekends kept me going, I loved partying with my friends, dancing like a deranged dervish on the dance floor, sending Martin for comedy size carry outs in the morning and ranting about football to Davie, Tony and Martin. This lifestyle had two main effects. Firstly, my employers at Salvesen's were getting annoyed with my attitude and, with hindsight now, I see that they were trying to get me sacked, but that they needed me for the time being and when I got going I was a good worker. Secondly, the lifestyle of all the years of partying, all the nonsense and all my unresolved issues regarding the break up of my family when I was a boy ensured that when I met the most amazing woman I have ever met, I wasn't in the best mental state to cope with it. Falling in love with Shelley put my brain in to overload, though I was, of course, blissfully happy with her.

When she asked about my family I gave the typical response I always gave that usually shut people up. I should have told her the truth. She would have been the first person I had ever told. I tried to tell her the truth once when we were out for a walk one night, but fate intervened and I was beaten up by four younger guys over a silly comment the night England beat Scotland 2 - 0 in the first leg of the Euro 2000 qualification play-off. If she hadn't been there to ask them to stop I think I would've been kicked to death. That fight buggered my head up even more as I was now paranoid about recriminations, and now only left the house to go to work, attend football matches or to go clubbing. I was a mental wreck, so this of course made me drink even more.

I don't want to discuss my relationships with Maria and Shelley any further out of respect for them both, and also because I'm embarrassed and ashamed of some of the things I said and did whilst drunk. Suffice to say that Shelley and I lasted until February 2000, when she finished with me. I was utterly distraught at having lost her, but with hindsight I see that she deserved more than a drunken idiot like me. I doubt I'll ever meet such a wonderful girl again. It was the only time I ever looked forward to getting home from work, just so I could see her. I hope she is really happy; she deserves to be. I was utterly destroyed when we split up, and I was also sacked from my job at Salvesen's a few weeks before, though I had got another job straight away.

Martin was very supportive towards me when all this happened, despite the tricky situation he was in being both her brother and my friend but, like the thing with my parents, I felt I couldn't talk to anyone about how I felt. It must have appeared that I didn't give a toss, as I avoided the subject completely. However, I'm not the first person to fuck up a relationship with someone they love and I doubt I'll be the last, and it's taught me that if I ever become involved in such a relationship again I won't let go. I met two beautiful women and loved them both, in different ways. Something many men aren't lucky enough to ever experience.

Chapter 5
Downward Spiral

After the millennium I let myself go big time. I started smoking dope, something that rarely interested me before, but it now seemed to ease the pain. I still felt guilty about the way I had moved from one woman to the other so quickly and about any hurt I had caused them. I was also in debt up to my eyeballs now as my new job didn't pay as well as my old one. The stuff in my head about my family still gnawed away at me and I even let my appearance go. It took my good mate Davie to tell me that 'you stink' to snap me out of it a bit. To be blunt, life was getting on top of me. My old employer and friend, Andy, was kind enough to take me on again at BFD, so I had a little bit more money. Enough to still go out with Davie, Tony and the lads every couple of weeks.

Nights out now were almost entirely just about the drink, drugs and music, though we still had some fantastic nights in 2000, most notably ATB and Paul Oakenfold at Room at the Top. Davie and Jenny had a wee boy on 6 February 2000 and called him Marc.

Hibs were of great comfort to me in 2000, though they predictably ruined my birthday by losing the Scottish Cup semi-final to a very poor Aberdeen side 2-1 after leading 1-0, thanks to a brilliant solo effort from Russell Latapy. My birthday (7 April) always coincides with Scottish Cup semi-finals, not a good thing if you're a Hibs fan as we haven't won the trophy since 1902.

All this time it was weed during the week and drink at the weekend. The people at BFD must have noticed a big difference in me compared to the first time I worked there. It's strange, though, that if you work and get smashed all the time people just think you like a drink or are a party animal, whereas people on the dole who do the same thing get labelled wasters. It's a fine line.

Hollie, by now Martin's ex and still a good friend of mine, moved in with me in the summer of 2000 as she had come down from Livingston from uni in Dundee to work for the summer. I liked having her stay, though my mate Martin didn't come up as much when she was around. I started seeing Maria again for a while just when she came home for the odd weekend, but by now that vile weed had seriously messed with my brain. I ruined my friendship with Hollie by allowing our relationship to become a bit more than just friends, which was a mistake. We were attracted to each other, but to be honest I was still upset about losing you-know-who and this, coupled with cannabis induced mood swings, ensured that we fell out and she moved back up to Dundee. Understandably, I wasn't to hear from her or Maria again until fairly recently, I think they have forgiven me, at least I hope they have. Relationships aside, they are two of the best friends I have ever had.

Curiously, after this episode with Hollie, weekends started to be fun, but for entirely different reasons. Tony and Davie would be away playing golf while Martin and I went to watch Hibs or got wasted at home. I still really missed Shelley, but the mad nights we started having were therapeutic. Saturday night without fail would see me, Martin, Davie, Tony and Jenny having a 'few drinks' then heading down to mine when Jenny went to bed, as she was usually up early with their wee boy Marc. Though my friends in the past have had kids, Davie and Jenny were the first mates I had where I knew the kid basically from day one. It was fascinating over the years seeing the wee boy grow from a tiny bundle on the couch to a crawling, toddling, walking, talking little man.

The 'stagger' that me and the three lads made in the early hours of every Sunday morning from Davie's house in Ladywell to my own house about two miles away in Craigshill was never uneventful. Laden with joints and a huge carry out, we would amuse ourselves walking through the schemes by playing chap door run, hilarious, especially when the four of us had a combined age of over eighty. The Howden district we walked through to get to my bit got the worst of it, and eventually it became chap door walk away as we couldn't be bothered to run. We'd eventually get back to my house and start drinking again, the blaring hi-fi oscillating between pumping dance tunes and Irish rebel music, usually the Wolfe Tones or Shebeen. We were all Catholics and supported Hibs or Celtic, so we saw nothing wrong with this, especially as we all had genuine Irish ancestry.

The block of flats I lived in was one of five other blocks nearby and they all heard it too. They definitely all heard the rebel music when we opened my big living room windows and put the speakers outside, 5am in the morning and a good two hundred people were treated to 'boys of the old brigade', 'the merry ploughboy' or, if I was drunk enough to let them play it, the 'Celtic symphony'. Not only was this music blared at clubsonic volume in the early hours, but also we all drunkenly roared along with the lyrics as we knew them all, dancing around my living room stamping our feet and clapping our hands. What a bunch of lunatics we were.

Astonishingly, I only ever got one complaint in all the years I lived there. It was a first floor flat so Christ knows what poor Colin, the Hearts fan downstairs, made of it all. The one complaint was when some new guys moved into the flat directly upstairs from me. They were huns (Rangers supporters) and were obviously furious at the barrage of noise they were subjected to every weekend. They sent a local so-called hard man round to 'sort me out' one night but I was out with the lads and only my wee mate Martin was in my house. This thug, at least three times the size of Martin, hung him out of the window and asked him 'can you fucking fly?' before telling him we were to keep the noise down. We were shocked when Martin told us, but obviously not as shocked as the two guys upstairs. They had obviously banked on me being in when this giant came down to make threats. Now they knew I hadn't been in. And they knew I knew what they'd tried to do. That night the music blared louder than ever before. They shat it and moved out of the flat as soon as they could. No one else ever came to my door about the noise, but four drunk, shouting maniacs blaring rebel music must be scary, no matter how harmless we actually were. I still meet people today who used to live in that street and they are shocked when I tell them it was my mates and me.

The rebel music, the football and the partying made life fun and easier to handle, and this carried on for another year and a half. Tony and I had a fantastic day out at the 2001 Scottish Cup Final, even though Hibs lost 3-0 to a very strong Celtic side who were going for the domestic treble. Tony is a Celtic fan so we spent that day in Bairds, a notorious Celtic/Irish pub in Glasgow's Gallowgate. I was the only Hibs fan in this pub and received a god-like welcome for having the guts to wear my Hibs top. There was one weegie (Glaswegian) Celtic fan who obviously wanted a fight but I just ignored him and some other Celtic supporters put him out. I don't remember much about the game other than that we never managed a shot on target against Celtic, and the massive 'HAIL HAIL' I started when Tony and I walked into the Hibs end. Fair dues, Tony sat in the Hibs end with me, and the only ribbing I got was when Henrik Larsson scored Celtic's third and he gave me a dead leg. Hampden Park is generally a miserable place if you're a Hibs fan, especially that seemingly endless journey east back along the M8 after yet another Hampden howler.

Chapter 6
Catalogue Fraud

My debt was getting out of control now, and I owed thousands, probably over fifteen thousand with overdrafts, loans, bank charges, etc. Banks are evil. They just throw debt at you when you turn 18, 'have this', 'have that'. But when you go to see them to get help for your debt it's another story. To quote comedian Mark Walliams, 'computer says no'.

I tried to get myself out of the financial mess I was in by getting some mail order catalogues under a dodgy name, ordering stuff then selling it on, but I was caught for this and a report was sent to the procurator fiscal, the Scottish department of public prosecutions. Since I was basically caught red-handed I got most of the stuff back for the police, who were actually very nice to me and, instead of a summons, I was allocated a social worker to find out why I had done this.

I was shocked when the policeman asked how much smack I took. I've never touched that kind of shit and never will, but I must have looked a right mess on the weed for him to think that. The social worker came up a few times and obviously saw that I had committed the crime out of desperation as I had a job, etc, and that was the end of the matter, though it was kept on my record. The downside of this was that I had to agree to contact all the companies involved, admit to the fraud and get the bills changed into my own name. I was told that I could actually have all the goods back once I had done this so I would at least be able to sell them again and get some cash, but the confiscated items were never returned to me and I was left with yet another huge bill.

In August 2001 I resolved to get myself a better-paid job to help get me out of the mess I was in. I initially applied to Debenhams Warehouse, as the money was good. I sat through an awful three hour team building interview before they told us the job involved Saturday night shifts, at which point I politely told them I wasn't staying sober at the football for anyone. I also applied to 3663 at Newbridge, on the advice of my mate Davie. The money was good (£340 a week) and the hours suited my lifestyle, so I applied and was given an interview. This interview was more like the ones I was used to, the manager asking about my experience and willingness to do overtime, a common thing in distribution. I thought I had done well but wouldn't hear until the next Wednesday.

My reason for wanting to leave BFD a second time wasn't purely financial. Though my immediate superiors at BFD, Alex, Andy and Del were really sound and good to work for, the company's owner had recently appointed a new general manager whom I'll call Robert. Straight away I knew that this new general manager was a bigot and a fanny. He pulled a workmate of mine up for wearing a Celtic hat, declaring 'I'm a Hamilton Academical fan'. Then I heard the clown a few days later going on about Rangers. Hamilton Accies my arse!

Things came to a head with him one Thursday when we were short staffed and he knew we had a very busy weekend ahead. He wanted us all to come in and work on the Saturday for single time to cover the extra workload. I and all the lads crammed into his office to tell him we weren't up for this at all, but he eventually bullied everyone except me into agreeing. 'We've got Rangers at Ibrox on Saturday and I'm going, so I'm not working, Robert,' I said. I was lying. I was planning to watch the game on Sky with my mates, but that was none of his business. He tried to act the big man by telling the lads to leave the office, then asking me to stay behind while they were still in earshot. I think he thought he was going to make an example of me.

'You will work Saturday, Ian,' he said.

'Nope,' I replied. 'I told you, I'm busy.' I offered to work late on the Friday instead, but he continued

'How long have you worked here?' he asked.

'About 16 months this time around,' I coolly replied.

'I don't think you'll be working here much longer if I'm anything to do with it,' he threatened.

I gave him the cheesiest sarcastic smile I could muster and replied 'RIGHT. OK.'

He asked me to leave the office and advised me to look for another job. What a fucking Arsehole. Little did he realise that I had had my 3663 interview only a couple of days before.

I didn't work the Saturday, in fact if I remember correctly it didn't go ahead. I sat with the lads and watched Tam McManus fire Hibs into an early lead before Rangers got back into it, leading us 2-1 until Alen Orman smashed in a superb equaliser from outside the box to end the game at two all. A great result for Hibs, a poor one for Rangers.

I took gleeful delight in asking my 'manager' if he had enjoyed the game when Monday came. I had another surprise for him too. That Wednesday, while at work, I phoned 3663 to see if I had got the job. I had got it! I was to start the very next Sunday night. That felt sweet and I walked through to the warehouse jubilantly singing 'cheerio, cheerio, cheerio' before writing out a deliberately crude letter of resignation and barging into the manager's office.

'I've got another job, like you said, and I'm leaving this week,' I told him flatly.

'Oh no you're not,' he replied. 'You'll work a month's notice or I'll get accounts to freeze your bank account.' Now I knew this guy really was a fanny, I knew he couldn't do that, and as we had just been paid he couldn't even hold onto my last wage or deduct from it.

'Nah, I don't think so,' I said to him, in possibly the most disrespectful tone I have ever spoken in. He went purple in the face and started ripping up my resignation before telling me to get out of the office. We were very short staffed as it was and his little plan had blown up in his face. I was itching to tell him that my mate Davie, who also worked with me, was also trying to get a job in 3663 but I thought I'd better leave that particular pleasure for Davie himself. In the end I didn't even finish that week, I just walked out after an hour of the next day's shift, leaving all my work to be finished by others. They were probably a little miffed at that but they were all good lads and understood why I had done it.

Hilariously, not only myself, but Davie, our shift manager Alex and most of the company's drivers soon also left for the better pay and conditions of 3663 and, to add insult to injury, 3663 pinched a lot of BFD's customers too. I wasn't bothered about that, BFD's owner Mr Reilly was a decent and sound man, and I'm sure he would have emptied that nasty manager who drove us all out if he had known what he was doing to his staff. I pitied those left behind to work under this bully, but Mr Reilly eventually did empty him. Anyway, I had a really well paid job now and was eager to get cracking at 3663 and hopefully to give my life a kick-start.

Chapter 7
Flatmates

You may remember that all this time, since late 1998, I have been friends with Martin. In the summer of 2001 someone we knew convinced him to grow a cannabis plant in his spare room, promising Martin wads of cash when the 'crop' was ready to harvest. I saw the plant once in its later stages and without any exaggeration it was like a palm tree, with a full hydroponics set up. Unfortunately, Martin was never to see any money that came from the plant as the grower kept it all for himself. The damp caused by the plant ruined Martin's flat too. To make matters worse he was being hounded for council tax debt, and to be honest I think his housing officer had it in for him. His parents had sadly both died by the time he was 20 or 21 and he didn't work, so his options were a bit limited when he was evicted.

I asked Martin to move into my spare room as my lodger. I paid full rent as I worked, so the dole paid me £168 per month rent for him, but he is my mate and I would have let him move in whatever the financial circumstances. He stayed at my house a lot of the time anyway after we had all been out or when he was too pissed to walk home, so it was the logical thing to do. He gave me somewhere to stay in 1998 when Eric and I were evicted from the old flat so I wasn't going to let him down. The weed had also made me very paranoid about being burgled whilst I was out on nightshift, though I also had good reason to be as there had been a lot of break-ins in my area at that time, so having my mate move in meant there was always going to be someone in the flat.

My new job was brilliant, the hours, the money and the people all suited me perfectly. Indeed this was the first company I ever worked for who knew how to take care of its employees. Davie soon started back beside me and we had a great crack with all the lads, driving around the warehouse listening to pumping club music on Beat 106 while we worked, often stoned. I never smoked cigarettes so I didn't understand nicotine addiction, and when I got cravings I thought my brain was craving a joint not a fag, so I often went to work a little stoned, as did much of the workforce, except Davie. The job itself was as boring and monotonous as all my other jobs had been, though it was easy. I had money to live a little again too with my improved wages and, coupled with the rent I got from Martin, this meant I could start going out again and going wild.

That September I bought a PlayStation 2 and this provided us all with hours of entertainment playing football games, in which I always went Hibs, of course. I also attended my favourite ever Hibs game round about this time. As usual Martin and I took our place on the East Stand for the visit of local rivals Hearts. We had enjoyed quite a good run against them with Alex Mcleish as manager, only losing to them once during his reign so far.

It wasn't the match itself that was memorable, Hibs were 2-0 up at half time thanks to two goals from our Ecuadorian wingback, Ulises De La Cruz, and we won 2-1 despite Hearts scoring a consolation late on. It was the atmosphere. Our fans, and particularly those in our stand, were well up for it. From the kick off right up until the very last second we sang, roared and chanted all of our songs at the miserable Hearts contingent in the away end, including a one off 'Happy birthday 6-2, we only fucked you 6-2, happy birthday dear jambos, happy birthday 6-2' as it was a year since we had destroyed them by that score line in a live Sky match at Easter Road in front of the whole of Britain. Just as importantly, every time Hearts got the ball we booed, whistled and jeered and obviously made their players bottle it. This kind of booing usually only lasted the first twenty minutes of the derby game, but on this occasion we kept it up for the whole game.

The atmosphere was white hot. At the final whistle, our skipper Franck Sauzee and the rest of the team came over to give the East Stand a big round of applause and we gave them a standing ovation back. If ever the term 'twelfth man' used to describe the effect fans can have on a game is appropriate, it is appropriate when discussing this game.

And so 2001 drew to a close with a few fantastic nights out just like the old times, many a dance music and rebel music session in my house and lots of games of football on the PS2, punctuated by the odd one night stand to stop myself from going mad, though I hadn't fancied anyone properly for ages now other than, ironically, a Hearts-supporting girl from Gorgie I saw for a few weeks. Entwined in all this was monotonous work, heavy drinking and partying. I had a disastrous relationship with a neighbour in early 2002, and there was some other hassle when I lost my debit card one night and someone used it at the local garage. Never go out with a neighbour, the effects can be disastrous.

I moved on to late night shifts early in 2002 and this opened my eyes a bit to what my flatmate was doing while I was at work. I honestly never knew how much he drank until he lived with me. I used to think that when he went home to his place after a weekend at mine he just laid low like the rest of us, but he was drinking by himself.

I'd never met anyone who drank alone to the extent Martin did. It was, of course, his business but I started to get paranoid whilst at work about what he might be doing in the house while having his one man piss ups, whether it be blaring out music or letting people in that he shouldn't have. I tried to talk to him about this but all he said was, 'It's just my way.' I know better now of course, like me, he was an alcoholic, and perhaps that's why his heavy drinking alone annoyed me so much, it reminded me of how I could end up.

Two alcoholics in one house is a bad idea. The weed didn't help with this situation, as it makes you worry more if you are already stressed, but I dearly wanted to stop. It was nigh on impossible as absolutely all of my friends smoked it too. I couldn't even have a quiet weekend in to straighten up, as everyone still came to mine on a Saturday to get wrecked and, though I loved seeing my mates, I really needed some time out as I felt as though I was cracking up. Even if I tried to tell people I wanted a quiet weekend, they would've just said they were coming to see Martin so there wasn't much I could do.

Chapter 8
Decision Time

I did warn Martin that if his drinking didn't stop he would have to find somewhere else to live, but understanding alcoholism the way I do now I know that it wasn't going to be as simple as that for him. I think me giving him a hard time about drinking actually made him worse. I found empty White Lightning bottles out in the street, under his bedroom window and a load of empty sherry and cider bottles in his room once when I went in to investigate a nasty smell. He also woke me up a few times when I was sleeping off a nightshift by playing shooting games loudly on the PS2 whilst drinking, and that was the final straw.

I told him to move out in May 2002 and he moved in with his brother Paul again, this time in Paul's flat down the road. Martin and I are the best of mates and I'd do anything for the guy, but I wouldn't recommend sharing a house with a friend to anyone, no matter how well you usually get on, as you will only have fall outs. I'll certainly never share a house with a good mate again. Don't get me wrong, most of the time Martin lived with me was a right laugh, wasted all the time, making prank phone calls, listening to music and setting the world to rights. It was the drinking thing that ruined the arrangement. You could say I've a cheek, as I've been as bad as that in the past on drink, but to be honest it was life that was getting to me, and Martin's drinking was just the straw that broke the camel's back.

He moved out and I went to see the doctor to get help with my hash problem. He gave me Valium to take twice a day and at first they seemed like the answer. They seemed to blast away all my fears, paranoia and neurosis and I was able to go around smiling again for a while. However, I still didn't understand that I was now addicted to nicotine and I still ended up smoking a little, not as much, but still enough to pickle my head. Eventually I got sick of the Valium and dished them all out to mates at a party for a laugh to get rid of them. I'm amazed I managed to hold down a full time job in that state, but I did.

I still missed one of my ex's even now. I still hadn't seen or contacted my dad for over ten years and I hadn't been to see my grandparents in ages. I still saw my mum and sister, whom I got on brilliantly with, though I only saw them a couple of times a week at most due to my strange working hours and weekend lifestyle. The debt was getting me down too, which only made me even more stressed.

The final nail in the coffin of my life in Livingston came in June 2002 when I was charged with a minor breach of the peace offence. Though with hindsight this was superficial, it drove me round the bend with paranoia. I thought I was going to go to jail, what with my previous record for mail order fraud and a football related offence when I was sixteen. I also thought I was going to lose my job over the breach of the peace thing, which looking back was near paranoid delusion.

I had hired a PC from a local company and was using the Internet lots now, mostly to go in football chat rooms to wind people up but also to look into the possibility of doing a runner. My mate Tony suggested that if I were to do such a thing Ireland would be my best bet as they spoke English. I was a Catholic and I thought I knew a lot about the Republic. Tony, Davie, my mum, in fact everyone tried to get me to chill out about the breach of the peace thing, telling me there was no way I would go to prison, but in my head I had blown it out of all proportion. Anyway, it wasn't just that, I wanted a fresh start, away from all the bad memories of the incidents and relationships I have earlier described. I gave up my flat and moved back in with my mum for a while whilst I decided what to do. I was also going to have to give up a bloody good job.

I felt a bit more relaxed when I moved back into my mum's, but I looked damn awful. My hair had started to recede and I had shaved it down to a number 2. I had also lost a lot of weight. I was like a skeleton, mostly caused by stress.

Through my new PC I applied for a few jobs in the Irish Republic, and to my surprise I was offered a supervisor's position with a warehouse in County Galway. Unfortunately this all fell through at the last minute, but I did get one other job I had applied for. A guy called Neil from a company called Unibev telephoned me after receiving my CV and gave me a telephone interview. It seemed I was just the type of guy he was looking for in his busy beverages distribution unit. The guy was sound and, after asking why I wanted to move, he made a fair offer. If I could get to Ireland by 18 August 2002 I could start right away, initially on 370 euro a week, less cash than I was used to but it was a day shift and I was planning on living quietly, so I accepted.

Arranging accommodation was just as easy via the Internet as finding a job, and I wisely decided to live in a B&B initially so as to make things less stressful for myself. I soon had this arranged too, this time via telephone. My mum wasn't happy that I was going, but when she saw that my mind was made up she gave me some good advice. The same can be said of my friends.

Martin and I went to what was going to be our last Hibs game together, against Everton in a pre season friendly at Easter Road which finished two all, a young sixteen year old Everton striker you may have heard of called Wayne Rooney scoring one for The Toffees. I told a few people at work and others that I was actually moving to Holland in case the debt collectors tried to track me down.

So I was going to move to the Irish Republic. Now the only two problems I had were getting over there and getting some cash together. My family helped me the best they could and I had a little money put by from my sick pay (I was off work with stress for most of my last month with 3663) but I was banking on getting my holiday pay from 3663 when I left. Unfortunately, I misjudged the amount I was due and was left precariously short on funds for moving away. I just had enough and no more. The problem of actually getting to the Republic was solved when Tony offered to drive me over in his works van via an Irish Sea ferry. It was all sorted.

My last night out with the lads before I went had been to see Roger Sanchez at the Liquid Room in Edinburgh a couple of months before I left. It was a cracking night. The week before I left, Davie and Jenny had a housewarming party at their new house in Craigshill that also doubled up as my leaving party. It was a good night, though obviously I was upset at the thought of never doing this kind of thing with them again. I did see two last Hibs games on the television, both Sunday games, both defeats, going down 5-1 away to Hearts and losing 4-2 at home to Rangers. I had been too hung-over to attend these games, thankfully.

In the days prior to that Saturday when I left Craigshill for what I thought was forever, I had a lot of time to reflect on the first twenty-four years of my life, and I have also had ample time to reflect on it since. To be honest I've no real complaints. Though I wasn't going to miss the actual place, I was going to miss the people whom I had grown up with, my friends and of course my family. Up to now I might have given the impression that I am either an idiot or a loser and, though I've said and done things I regret, I look back on my old life in Livingston mostly with fondness. I do not have a single problem with anyone I have mentioned so far and I've no axe to grind with anyone featured thus far. Life is too short and, despite the problems I had with debt, etc, I was just basically a normal guy who liked a party. I've had a lot of girlfriends, mostly short term because I was immature, but I've only mentioned the important ones or those relevant to my leaving the country.

Chapter 9
Cheerio

The train slowly came to a halt at Edinburgh Waverley. It was one thirty in the afternoon and we were cutting it fine. Edinburgh is a busy city centre to try and run through at the best of times, but half past one on a hot and sunny Saturday afternoon on the first day of the new football season is just pandemonium.

Darren and I finished the bottles of Buckfast tonic wine that we had been drinking on the train and started to make our way through the heaving mass of people on the platform towards the far end of the train station, where the steep steps would take us out onto Leith Street. Time was of the essence. Although we had both drunk a bottle of wine each on the way through and were feeling pretty drunk, we wanted to grab a quick pint or three in the Hibs Supporters Club before heading for the stadium.

We made our way down Leith Street, past the playhouse, determined to reach a suitable watering hole before we took our places on the East Stand. We passed quite a few Aberdeen fans as we bounded down London Road towards Easter Road, home of my beloved team. Aberdeen was the team we were playing today, but on this occasion we had neither the time nor the desire to wind them up. All we wanted was a pint.

As we made our way along London Road and came to the junction that takes you down Easter Road, I looked down and saw a sight that always made my heart glow with pride. Apart from the odd little dot of red and white, which indicated the presence of some away fans, Easter Road was a seething mass of green and white. Hibs supporters of all shapes and sizes, ages and sexes.

Usually the mere sight of this was enough to start me singing one of our songs, but today I felt somewhat different. It was a melancholy site rather than an awe inspiring one, and my feeling this way had nothing to do with the fortified wine I had gulped down earlier. Darren and I made our way through the crowd down Easter Road, checking out some of the multitude of gorgeous Hibby lassies as we went, but this time there was no cheeky chat up line, no making eye contact. We bashed and dodged our way through until we reached Sunnyside Lane, where we turned right and headed down the steep cobbled road towards the Hibernian FC Supporters Association Club.

The doormen let us in despite us being a little worse for wear, and we made our way to the bar where I bought us two pints each and a double whisky. The cue was bloody massive, as usual. Darren, already quite drunk as he wasn't as hardened a party animal as me, looked warily at the bumper round that I had bought, but then laughed and we soon had these drinks tanned. Twenty past two. We had made good time, though my spindly legs were aching from all the dodging in and out of crowds. Our drinks finished, we quickly squeezed through the busy club and out of the big double doors and staggered towards the stadium. I was absolutely hammered by now, so God knows what state Darren was in.

We swaggered along Albion Road towards the entrance to the East Stand at Hawkhill Avenue. I had a season ticket, but Darren had a normal ticket for the game so we stood in different queues. I looked at my new season ticket that had cost me the best part of three hundred quid. I tore out the relevant voucher and handed it to the lass behind the turnstile.

'A fat lot of good this is going to do me,' I thought to myself as I put it back into the pocket of my Firetrap designer jeans and scrambled up the steep steps that led on to the East Stand. I was up them in a jiffy, taking two steps at a time, and was joined there by Darren. The ground was already filling up, with a sizeable away support. Darren's ticket was actually for a different block of seats but my own seat had a big empty space beside it where whoever was accompanying me to games would normally just stand, like we all did. East Stand, row V, seat 100. Right up the back, under the TV gantry. The best seat in the stadium. In fact, to me it was the best seat in the world. It was here, with my Hibby friends, that we led the vocal support and started nearly all of the intimidating songs that helped our beloved team overcome whoever its opponents might be. The fact that I rarely, if ever, sat on that seat which I had occupied for many years or that I had to clamber over various rows of seats to get to it, mattered little. This is where we stood and sang and watched our team. This was my church. This was where I healed my hurt.

The two teams, Hibs in green and white, Aberdeen in all red, left the field after their warm ups and that was our signal to start. Grabbing the railing of the overhead walkway to my left so as to gain extra leverage in my voice, I bellowed the words that were ingrained into my brain, 'HAIL, HAIL, THE HIBS ARE HERE.' Darren and two thousand other voices helped me finish the song in unison, 'ALL FOR GOALS AND GLORY, ALL FOR GOALS AND GLORY, HAIL, HAIL THE HIBS ARE HERE, ALL FOR GOALS AND GLORY NOW.'

The whole stand seemed to shake as the sound reverberated around it. The East Stand was where I always sat. It was the only part of the stadium that hadn't recently been turned in to one of those big two-tier soulless stands so common in Britain after Lord Taylor bizarrely decided to blame some sad football disasters in the 1980s on stadium design rather than on the failure to police the situation properly. The stand was basically a large covered terrace with seats in, but not many of us sat down: we preferred to stand as we always had done.

A fellow Hibby to my right started another song, aimed at the Aberdeen fans that poked fun at a popular stereotype of Aberdonians. 'SHEEP SHAGGING BASTARDS, YOU'RE ONLY SHEEP SHAGGING BASTARDS' we all roared in unison to everyone's mirth. It may not sound very intelligent or sophisticated in the cold light of day, but when you're plastered and you're with your mates, it's hilarious. The Aberdeen fans responded in their typical manner by singing the song back at us, in a painfully transparent attempt to pretend that having this sung to them every single week doesn't bother them, when it clearly does otherwise they wouldn't sing it back to us at all. Playground stuff really, but it DOES annoy them. This vocal sparring was interrupted by the arrival on the pitch of the teams. Aberdeen ran out first, to a chorus of boos, jeering and sheep noises from the home support that was only ended when our Hibernian heroes in green and white took to the field.

For such a big occasion, I was in a strange mood. Although we had a home game against the hated and despised Glasgow Rangers in a fortnight, I knew that this would probably be my last visit ever to see my beloved Hibs at Easter Road. I was moving away to the Irish Republic in a few weeks and the game against 'the Huns' had been moved to a Sunday to accommodate BBC Scotland, a Sunday that was the day after one of my best mate's house warming parties. The chances of me making that game were negligible, as the house warming had also turned into my own leaving party. I'd either still be up or be comatose in my bed when the Rangers game kicked off. So this would be my last game. Hibs had basically been shite for over a year since our boss Alex McLeish had left for Rangers. One of our best players ever, Franck Sauzee, had quickly become our worst manager ever, being sacked after less than seventy days and who had been replaced with Bobby Williamson, it seemed to me that man had never heard of the term 'attacking football'.

Burnt

I looked around the stand at those comrades who had stood shoulder to shoulder with me for many a year. Darren was quiet, probably from the drink. I had a tear in my eye but managed to hold it back and shout for joy as our Spanish striker, Paco Luna, put us one nil up. The usual bedlam that followed a Hibs goal ensued in the stands around me as we all jumped up and down, singing and dancing to our wee ditty 'lets all do the hibeesbounce, nananananananana'. Maybe it wasn't going to be such a bad season. The manager wasn't very popular but at least he could organise a team.

We went in at half time 1-0 up thanks to Paco's goal, and I ate my last ever Easter Road pie. By now I had the thirst for more drink but wasn't going to leave early on my last ever trip to the holy ground. The second half got underway and we seemed to have the best of it, though Aberdeen were ominously coming back into the game. The guy who stood on the other side of the gantry passed me a grass joint, which I had one take from and passed back. Aberdeen equalised. Time was running out and it looked like the game was heading for a draw, but myself and obviously a lot of other Hibs fans had that familiar 'sinking feeling' as Aberdeen pinned us back in the closing stages. Surely my last ever Hibs game wasn't going to end in an ignominious defeat like this? Darren Mackie confirmed our fears by scoring the winner for Aberdeen with only minutes remaining.

'Fuck's sake,' I thought. 'What a last game to see.' Hibs 1-2 Aberdeen. I briefly explained to the lads who stood near me that I was going away and wasn't coming back. They all shook my hand and wished me luck, Darren and I trudged depressingly back up towards Waverley and the train that would take us home to Livingston.

The trip home was as uneventful as the Hibs match, and Darren and I popped into the old Copper Ton Bar in Livingston when we got off the train. After another few pints we bumped into some Celtic fans I knew and sat with them, finding great amusement in annoying patrons with a cheesy Martin O'Neil mask. One of the lads, Gareth, asked how I was getting on and where I was working. I informed him that I was moving to the Irish Republic in a few weeks and that I had been on 'sick leave' from my job at 3663 Food Distribution for a few weeks with stress.

Gareth said, 'That sounds a bit drastic, Ian, why are you moving over there?'

Chapter 10
The Big Move

I said goodbye to my mum and sister on the Saturday morning before Tony and I loaded my stuff into his blue LDV Cub works van. I was limited as to what I could take as I didn't know how big my room at the B&B was going to be. In the end I took most of my clothes, about two hundred CDs, a small CD player which I had swapped with my mum for my hi-fi, a washing basket and a sixteen inch colour television. In a cardboard box I packed all my personal stuff, photos, the key ornament given to me when I turned eighteen, two little cards given to me by an ex and all my old certificates and documents. My mum had given me a St Christopher thingy and I resolved to keep that on me at all times, St Christopher being the patron saint of safe travels.

And so the travelling began. I had the ferry booked for early afternoon, but we left early-ish on the Saturday morning as the M8 motorway had road works on it meaning we had to take a less direct route across Scotland. I honestly don't remember the exact route Tony drove to Stranraer as I was far too busy thinking about what I was doing and listening to Tony giving me little pieces of advice on how to look after myself. I would hopefully arrive in Dundalk by around 6pm.

The drive to Stranraer ended up taking absolutely ages due to the relatively poor roads. We missed the ferry I had booked but as I hadn't paid for it yet we were able to catch the next one, in theory anyway. For some bizarre reason I was worried that either the police or the debt collectors would be waiting for me when we tried to board the ferry, which of course was utter nonsense.

I was soon panicking as we eventually drove up to board the ferry though, for entirely different reasons. As we stopped at the kiosk where you paid or handed over your ticket, the guy in the kiosk gave me some awful news. He informed me that as Tony's van was a works vehicle we would be charged at the commercial rate rather than the standard one, which would cost an extra eighty pounds cash. I was horrified. They hadn't mentioned this on the phone. That left me with hardly any money at all to do me until I got my first wage.

We bitterly argued with this clown, pointing out that we weren't going over there on business and therefore weren't commercial customers, even showing him all my belongings in the back, but he wasn't having any of it. It was an extra eighty quid or we weren't getting on the ferry. What was I to do? I had no job or flat to go back to, everything was arranged in Ireland and I would've looked a right idiot just going back to Livingston because of this. I'm sure the kiosk man could tell I was desperate to get away. Reluctantly I agreed to pay the extra money, which I'm sure the kiosk wanker just pocketed for himself as he didn't write anything else down or change my ticket. Tony thankfully reassured me that he could give me forty pounds, which was helpful, though I was still pretty skint and now very worried in case my new job was paid in arrears.

We drove into the bowels of the enormous P&O ferry that was to carry me across the Irish Sea to my new life. We got out of the van, bounding up the steep steps that take you on to the ferry. I had a lump in my throat as the ferry slowly sailed out of the big bay at Stranraer, out into a very choppy open sea.

The ferry trip itself was pretty uneventful and gave me time to doze away the slight hangover I had from the vodka I had drank the night before. Tony and I went outside onto the deck and climbed up a little, getting a fantastic view of the sea as the Isle of Man came into sight. I still had my old 3663 employee card and remembered that 3663 made up orders for both ferry companies who operated out of Stranraer. I blatantly used this card to blag myself and Tony a free meal and some drinks in the expensive on board restaurant. Lasagne and Budweiser for me. While on board I foolishly tried to phone one of my ex's to apologise and say goodbye, but I got her voicemail and bottled it, pretending to be one of my mates and just leaving a silly joke message instead. I don't know if she ever got it or if she even still had the same number by then.

As the ferry sailed into Belfast I took my first look at my new island, albeit the British controlled part. What an absolute dump it looked, though to be fair it looked mostly like disused dockyards. We disembarked at Belfast and were given directions to find the road to take us South, through Fermanagh and Armagh and across the border into Louth and ultimately Dundalk, which lay roughly halfway along the road between Belfast and Dublin.

Belfast was a very curious sight. All kinds of flags were erected in people's gardens. I saw Butcher's Aprons (Union flags), Tricolours, St Patrick's Cross flags, St George's Cross flags, Palestinian flags, Red Hand of Ulster flags and Israeli Star of David flags, among others. Tony and I commented how wild and intimidating all this looked and that I should be thankful that it wasn't here I was going to be working and living.

After getting lost a couple of times we eventually found the proper road to take us south. We were in a hurry for two reasons. Tony wanted to get back to his bird's house that night for a party but, more importantly, we were running late and if he was going to make it back up to Belfast for the last ferry after dropping me off we were going to have to shift, big time. And shift we did! It was near enough a straight road all the way down. When we drove through the Moroy Pass and crossed the border my mobile phone bleeped. I had a new message from speakeasy, the Irish equivalent of O2, my network. It welcomed me to the Irish Republic. I felt relieved and overjoyed to think I was finally safe. No debt collectors could get me here. The police wouldn't come looking for me for that breach of the peace thing here. I've rarely felt such relief in my life. I let out a big 'YEEEEEEEEEEEESSSSSSSSS' that made Tony grin.

Now all we had to do was find Dundalk and my digs. Time was of the essence and if Tony was going to make it back to Belfast in time for that last ferry I would have to be dropped of somewhere convenient in Dundalk from where I could get a taxi to my digs. We found Dundalk without any problems. We found an OK looking petrol station and asked the man who worked in it if I could keep my gear in his shop while I waited for a taxi. He agreed and even phoned me a taxi. Tony hugged me and gave me his luminous Celtic hat for my work, before jumping back in his van and zooming off back north to catch the late ferry home. I was now completely alone. Yet I felt optimistic about the future. I had a good job and somewhere to stay and I hopefully had enough money to tide me over. I had a fresh start.

There was some confusion with my taxi driver as to where he was actually supposed to be taking me but eventually, after phoning my digs, we found the place. I was flabbergasted. It was a beautiful, enormous, obviously fairly new, house, almost like a modern version of an old mansion, with huge gardens, a shed almost bigger than my old flat and a massive driveway both front and back. The taxi driver helped me into the house with all my stuff and left.

When we arrived my new landlady, Sheila, warmly greeted me. She looked to be in her 50s but I've never been very good at judging ages. She made me feel very welcome and offered me a cup of tea and a sandwich, which I gladly accepted. We discussed arrangements for my rent, meals and so on and agreed on the very fair price of one hundred euros a week (about sixty five pounds in real money). This included my breakfast and evening meals, which saved me a lot of hassle. The only thing I would have to take care of myself was my laundry and lunch, but since nearly every newsagent in the area sold a variety of hot food and there were plenty of reasonably priced launderettes about, this was no problem.

Sheila showed me to my room, which was up a few flights of steps. It was very small with a single bed but it was nevertheless spotless and nice. It also had a kind of large upward facing window that during the day would give me fantastic views of the mountains to the north on the border. Sheila told me that the house was split in two. She and her husband lived with their children in one half, while the rooms in the half I was in were used by apprentices and workers who visited the area as there was an FAS Training Centre there (Irish equivalent of the Job Centre). For the time being I had half this massive house to myself, including the cosy living room with TV and dining table. I was exhausted, so I bade my kind landlady goodnight and settled down for a well-earned sleep, travelling does certainly take it out of you. Tomorrow I would explore my new hometown.

Chapter 11
Settling In

I slept like the proverbial top that night and woke feeling refreshed. It was a beautiful sunny day and very warm. My landlady offered to drive me into town and show me around a bit, which was very kind of her. The house was at the very end of a street called Avenue Road and it looked a good mile or more into town so I was glad of the lift. Sheila pointed out all the useful places to me, like the launderette and local shops, before driving me through the town centre to show me what was there.

I was surprised at the size of the town. I had been expecting a small village, but the place looked about half the size of my old hometown Livingston. There were hundreds of pubs. Literally. I think at the time there were over one hundred and fifty pubs in the town, many with adjoining off-licences, which was something I hadn't seen before. The town cathedral was beautiful. Thinking that I had my bearings, I thanked Sheila and she dropped me off so that I could explore on my own a little bit.

It was early on Sunday afternoon and the place seemed quiet. Walking past a pub called Oscars I heard a lot of noise inside and, thinking it was a televised football match, I decided to check it out. It was actually the semi-final of the all Ireland Gaelic Football Championships, between Armagh and someone else. I'd never really been interested in any other sport than football before but since this was to be my adopted home I decided to try and get into it. It was actually pretty entertaining stuff and I thoroughly enjoyed the game.

After the match I took a walk up the town's main thoroughfare and it was then I noticed a huge building in the town's Clanbrassil Street. On close examination I saw it was a Gaelic theme bar. I needed no further invitation. Exciting as the Gaelic game had been, I needed to find out the Hibs score from yesterday and maybe there was a live game showing in here. I walked up the steps into the bar. Looking around I saw the place had a pool table, an ENORMOUS television and that the walls were covered in memorabilia.

There were only a couple of customers in, and two bar staff. One was a local lad about my age whom I later discovered was named 'Stevy', the other was a bit older than me, shorter, but built like a tank with a closely shaven head and some really cool Celtic tattoos. When I ordered a pint in my Scottish accent the older barman offered me his hand and introduced himself as 'Mick', which instantly made me think of a guy who scored important goals for Celtic against my beloved Hibs in the 1970s. I soon got talking to him about the town, the people, where I was going to be working, who I was staying with, etc, and I found him to be a sound guy. He gave me some invaluable advice about getting my social security number sorted quickly and he advised me not to go drinking in the town's Bridge Street area, something my landlady had also warned me of. He even bought me a pint and gave me a few games of pool which, to a guy on his own, miles from his friends, family and home, was much appreciated. All this way to Ireland and I ended up drinking with a Weegie! (Glaswegian). He told me that my landlady's husband was a detective but that information mattered little to me, I was just glad of a friendly face to talk to.

I found out that Hibs STILL hadn't won. They had lost 2-1 to Dundee at Dens Park the day before, despite taking the lead through Garry O'Connor and were now bottom of the SPL. Still, I had made myself an acquaintance if not yet a friend and I decided that the Gaelic bar would be my local from now on, particularly as it had BBC Scotland and therefore would be showing SPL games live.

My first full day in my new hometown was going well. I decided to leave after a couple of pints as I was still saving my money and had to start my new job the next morning, albeit at the leisurely time of 11am. I said goodbye to Mick and Stevy and decided it was time to go home.

As I got back down to the main street I realised something. I was completely lost. Though I had a business card for where I was staying with the address on it, I had no idea which way to walk to even get onto the right road. It was a horrible feeling being lost. Already though I saw encouraging signs in myself. Catching my reflection in a shop window I noticed that my hair had grown back in a little bit and the stressed look I had worn for the last few months was utterly gone. Without being bigheaded I actually looked pretty good in my Firetrap jeans and retro Brazil football top, even if I was still a little skinny for my height of six feet. Not that this would help me find my digs, I thought.

I walked a little further along Dundalk's main street and decided that the only way I was going to get home was to ask directions. The first two people I met were two girls, both not bad looking though they looked four or five years younger than me. I explained to them that I was new to the town and was completely lost and needed their help. They were most helpful and showed me what way to go, but they also asked me to go for a drink with them in their local, McManus's pub, which was not too far away. I readily accepted this invitation and went with them to a cosy little pub in the middle of what looked like a very old housing scheme, which I found out was called Seatown. We all sat out in the walled beer garden which had a lovely open fireplace and the two girls, Ciara and Lorraine, introduced me to some of their friends whilst also introducing me to something new, Smirnoff Ice on tap!

We all sat for a few hours and had a great laugh and, though both girls were lovely, it was clearly Ciara whom I fancied, and I sat beside her when Lorraine left. Ciara was stunning, half Irish and half Hispanic looking, and we kissed for ages while waiting for a taxi that was to drop us home. By this time it was very late and I was slightly the worse for wear, so Ciara decided to get the same taxi as me. People over there share taxis, sometimes sharing big ones between multiple passengers and it is a friendly practice that should be encouraged over here so as to avoid the traditional 2.00am 'taxi battles'.

Ciara and I swapped numbers before the big taxi dropped me off back at my digs. What a day. I had met a sound Scottish guy, found two nice pubs and pulled a gorgeous girl. If this was life in Dundalk I was going to love it here. And tomorrow I would start my new job in an alcohol/soft beverages warehouse. Things were on the up for Ian Colquhoun!

Chapter 12
My New Job

I awoke the next morning with an AWFUL hangover. My head was pounding, my mouth was like birdcage sandpaper and my stomach felt like a washing machine on a turbo spin. I had plenty of time before work, however, and didn't feel as depressed as I normally did when hung over. I knew my workplace was on Coes Road, which wasn't very far from where I stayed, and I had indeed been shown where it was both by the taxi driver and by my landlady.

I donned my old 3663 uniform for want of better work clothes and started what I thought would be a short walk to work. I turned right and was soon in the United Beverages yard where I stopped and asked a female employee for directions. I told her I was looking for Neil Mulligan, to which she replied, 'Oh, he's actually JK Warehousing, a subcontractor, you want to go out and turn left then keep walking and you'll come straight to it.' I thanked her and retraced my steps, out of the United Beverages plant and back along Coes Road towards a big industrial estate. One problem. The woman who gave me directions had meant I should go round the corner to the left, not left back out of the yard. I walked a good three miles through an industrial estate with a raging hangover, getting increasingly frustrated and worried about being late on my first day, before a kind soul whom I asked for directions told me to turn around and go back the way I had come.

Eventually I found the warehouse at the back of the plant (most of the building was a soft drinks factory) and introduced myself to the manager, my new boss, Neil. He wasn't that bothered that I had been late and I was doubled up with an experienced man called Paul who was to show me the ropes. The lads asked me a lot of questions and I told them all about my adventures the day before.

The job itself I had sussed within ten minutes. It was ridiculously easy. We drove very old electric pallet trucks and went around the relatively small warehouse with a list of products to pick and stack on the pallet for delivery the next day. The only things I had to learn were a few new products that the warehouses I had worked in in Scotland hadn't stocked, but that wasn't exactly difficult. The boss Neil, and all the lads were sound guys, they made me feel welcome and we had a good laugh. I had to bite my tongue at a few 'Scottish' jokes for the first few weeks until they got to know me better, but all in all it was a great job, by far the most laid back atmosphere of any job I have worked. All we had to do was pick the orders and go home, with the exception of Mondays which were hellishly busy, and Fridays when there wasn't much to pick so we were usually sent to the yard to sort empty bottles, a tedious task but we got away early on Fridays so that more than made up for the bottle sorting. Within a few weeks I was easily the best picker in the warehouse, so good that I was rarely doubled up with anyone as I could do it so quickly and accurately.

My first day complete, I went off back to my digs to have my dinner, chill out and have a well earned sleep. Sheila made me a delicious dinner, as she did every night I was living there, and I watched some crap on television before going to my bed. I had awful nightmares for the first two weeks I lived in Dundalk, which I now know were the effects of me stopping the hash when I left Scotland. They were horrific nightmares, I would wake up in tears some nights, but after two weeks they were gone, thank God.

I went out one night during my first week there, just to break up the week as we had finished early at work, having a few pints with my cool boss and his brother and watching Celtic's shock exit from the Champion's League at the hands of FC Basle of Switzerland. I took a wrong turn whilst walking home and ended up completely lost again, this time late at night so there would be no 'rescue' from Ciara and Loraine. I had to phone a taxi but there were two problems. They couldn't understand my accent on the phone and I didn't know where I was. Somehow they found me though and, looking back, that was a funny episode and I got home safely.

As I had feared, my new job was to be paid a week in arrears so things were tight but thankfully my kind landlady let me off with my rent until I was paid. I didn't have a bank account either as I didn't have sufficient identification, so Neil kindly paid me in cash the first week and then by cheque thereafter until I eventually managed to open a bank account a couple of months later.

As I was skint I didn't see Ciara again for a wee while, though I wanted to of course. We eventually went for a lovely Italian meal one night before going to see Scottish band Shebeen in the Gaelic bar. It was a good night, though I did my usual disappearing act when I got too drunk. That night I was pleased to meet Shebeen's singer, Alan. I had heard a lot of their songs and I expected a giant, but he was just a normal kind of guy, very down to earth and a good laugh. I even got him to phone my mates in Livingston on my mobile and introduce himself, which was funny. Mick asked me how I was getting on and I thanked him for all his advice.

I was loving it in Dundalk. Things were going well. I bought an international phone card so I could call home more cost effectively and soon filled my friends and family in on how my brilliant my new life was going. I missed them all but the phone card and the odd quick call on my mobile kept me in touch with them. I was also delighted to hear that Davie, Jenny and Tony were coming over to see me in September and would be taking digs where I was staying. I found the time to write to Martin and his brother to say sorry for throwing Martin out when I did and gave them my new mobile number (I was kindly given an Irish sim card on my first day at work by Paul) so they could keep in touch.

Chapter 13
Things Getting Better

By now my hair had grown back and I had it chopped into a French crop. I was starting to look my best again and I even put on a bit of weight thanks to the big dinners my landlady made for me every night. I looked and felt great. Sheila's husband had kindly given me a loan of a mountain bike so I could get to work faster and this was a great help, not just for giving me an extra ten minutes in bed every morning, but it also got me super fit cycling to work every day. I had even started playing football again with my workmates, which was great fun and thoroughly enjoyable. They even christened me with the nickname 'Jockser'. I qualified to become an Irish citizen earlier than some immigrants as I have Irish ancestry on both sides of the family. I fully intended to become an Irish citizen, such was the regard for which I held my new home.

My three friends came over for the weekend and it was fantastic to see them again. We basically went out on the Friday and Saturday, going to have a few in Mick's Gaelic bar and meeting up with the lovely Ciara and her friends in McManus's on the Friday, before attending someone's 21st back in the Gaelic bar on the Saturday. We avoided the town's only 'nightclub', Vicars, as I had been there with the lads from work once and its music policy was awful. It was more like an old fashioned dancehall and hardly played any proper dance music, though it was still absolutely mobbed at the weekends What a laugh we had, even singing football songs in the street as we made our way home. Everyone I had met in this town was so nice and friendly and I think my friends were relieved to see I was doing so well and that I had met a nice girl. They left early on the Monday morning to get their flight back from Belfast to Scotland, and that midweek I got a surprise phone call from Martin and Paul, who had just received my letter. It was great to hear from them.

By October the digs I was staying in were now full of workers and apprentices, all a little younger than myself, but they were good lads and I got on well with them. However, I was starting to think that maybe it was time that I moved into my own place and gave things a go on my own. I was still seeing Ciara but not very often as I was still low on funds a lot of the time.

At the end of October I thought I had found suitable digs from an advert in the local paper, the Argus. I went and checked out the room and, seeing the room was OK and had a big new double bed, I paid a small deposit and took it. It was in an area called Demense, which I knew nothing about, but it was really handy for the town centre. Unfortunately, I didn't check who else I was sharing with as they weren't at home when I came to view the place, nor did I check out the kitchen or bathroom properly. Nevertheless I warmly thanked Sheila for looking after me so well in my time at her house and bought her a 'thank you' card and a box of chocolates to show my appreciation. Sheila was almost like my adoptive auntie or mum while I stayed there and perhaps I should have stayed a bit longer and saved money for a better place, but by now I was so happy and confident that I wanted a crack at being independent again.

I quickly realised that the house I had chosen to move into was a filthy tip and that my new housemates, though nice men, were a lot older than me, meaning that we had little in common. My room was OK but the rest of the house was minging. I had made a big mistake in moving there. And now I was stuck there. In desperation I wrote to my dad, asking for financial help with a deposit for a new place, but I wasn't sure if he would be able to help me as he had already loaned me money to go in the first place after I had broken our years of non contact by letter, just before I left for Ireland. In the meantime I resolved to work my way out of this situation and asked Mick if I could have a part time job at the Gaelic bar. He kindly agreed to train me but said he would have to ask the pub's owner, a local businessman called Mr McGlynn, if this was OK.

And so I became a barman for the first time. I worked a few evenings and weekends as a trainee so as not to interfere with my full time job and, although I was getting the hang of it, I was starting to get very sore legs for some reason. These pains were not just random.

I was working in the bar one Sunday in November when Hibs were due to take on Hearts live on BBC Scotland, which the bar of course had. The game itself started well, Hibs going one up through our big Finnish striker Mixu Paatelainen, but Kevin Mckenna and 'ugly' Phil Stamp scored in the second half to give Hearts the win. Still no derby win for Hibs under Bobby Williamson.

Something interesting and positive did happen that night though. A guy named Liam came into the pub and he was looking for someone to share a house with him and his friend Kevin. Liam was about my age and I sussed him out to be a sound guy, and when I found out that the house was as close to my day job as my first digs had been, I asked him if I could move in. Mick confirmed that Liam was sound and I had nothing to worry about and, as Liam was a taxi driver, I was able to abandon the horrible digs I lived in and move in with them that night, in the town's Manydown Close, just off Red Barns Road. The house was stunning, four bedrooms, living room, dining room, two bathrooms and a huge kitchen. Even the laminate flooring had heating underneath. It was like a mansion compared to where I had been staying. I went for a couple of drinks with my new housemates that evening and found them to be good guys, basically into the same things as me, beer, women, music and football! I really had landed on my feet now!

Meanwhile things at my day job were going well. I got a pay rise to four hundred euros a week and I also got all my tax back, around six hundred euros, meaning I could buy some much needed new clothes for going out at weekends. I was worried for a while when we were told our depot would be losing some work to our Dublin depot after Christmas, meaning that some of us were to be made redundant, but knowing my precarious financial position, my boss Neil soon took me aside and told me that I wasn't being paid off, not just because I was in a different situation to my colleagues but because I was the best picker. That was such a relief. I felt bad for the lads who were paid off, but it was done fairly on a last in first out basis, so no one could complain.

I was feeling really happy and secure now. I had two jobs, albeit my bar job was still on a trial/training basis and I had finally found somewhere perfect to stay with two likeminded guys, who quickly became good friends of mine too. We had some great nights out in town and some even cooler parties back at our luxury house. Indeed, the only thing going wrong was Hibs continuing to be piss poor. I saw two Hibs games other than that derby match whilst over there. A narrow CIS cup exit to Rangers at Easter Road (2-3) and an even narrower 1-0 home defeat to Celtic, Stilian Petrov scoring for them, a game which my new flatmates playfully ripped me about.

Chapter 14
Tomfoolery And Strange Goings On

The evening that Celtic played Blackburn Rovers in their first leg UEFA cup-tie at Celtic Park I ended up in a pub called the Train Down in Dundalk's Main Street with my workmates, as I hadn't been required to work that evening. We ended up in the pub until closing time, singing football songs and generally having a laugh, but certainly not annoying anyone. We were asked to leave but still took about twenty minutes to vacate the premises, though there was no trouble going on, it was all good natured. I thought little of it as I went and got myself a chippy and got a taxi home. I didn't know Mr McGlynn, the same businessman who owned the Gaelic bar I worked in, owned the Train.

Next morning I had to go into town before work and I stopped in at the Train to apologise for all the singing my mates and I had done the night before. There was only a barmaid on and she told me not to worry about it, that they had seen far worse in the pub and that my friends and I weren't barred. That was a relief. I was supposed to be working that night in the Gaelic bar for a benefit 'do' that was on and that I had been selling tickets for, both at work and about town, as a favour to Mick. Curiously, every time I tried to sell anyone a ticket for this benefit night I got a lot of funny looks from people. Some bought three or four, some refused, some bought but strangely said they wouldn't be attending. It was weird. It was as if there was something about these tickets that was either funny or sinister and it only seemed to be me who didn't know what. I sold about ten and gave the money to Mick and didn't try to sell anymore, handing the rest back.

When I arrived to work that Friday night in the bar I was shocked to find an attractive barmaid working beside the man who had replaced Stevy, whose name was Adrian. I asked them where Mick was but all I got was funny looks, just like when I tried to sell the benefit night tickets. I asked again where Mick was and still got no reply, and when I asked if I was still needed to work tonight I was told no. I didn't understand. I asked when Mick was coming back and still got no reply and more funny looks. What the fuck was going on? I had clearly been sacked for no reason. I wasn't barred though and Adrian poured me a pint while I texted around to make alternative arrangements for the evening. Something very strange was going on.

To be honest, working all those hours had made my sore legs even sorer and in a way I was glad to have the weekends back to myself. I got myself a lovely white designer jacket from a store in town and had another few good nights out with the lads in town, followed by parties back at mine. Pulling women certainly wasn't a problem. I don't know if it was my accent, my looks or the fact I was just a new face, but my old confidence returned. I even snogged my housemate Kevin's sister one night after we had all been out, which he didn't seem to mind. She was a lovely girl.

On Saturday, 14 December 2002 we had our works Christmas night out in Dundalk. We were in a few bars before we ended up in O'Brien's bar. It wasn't just a night out but a chance to say goodbye to those unfortunate enough to be getting paid off at Christmas. A great night was had by all and we were having such a good time. I was a little bit sad about not being able to go home for Christmas, but my housemate Liam had invited me to his family's place, which was really nice of him. It was outside this pub that I met Girl X (I'm not naming her out of respect).

Chapter 15
Girl X

She was absolutely gorgeous with short-ish blonde hair, piercing blue eyes and a figure to die for. I was attracted to her instantly. We introduced ourselves and kissed before realising that the bald bouncer wasn't going to let us back into O'Brien's as it was too late. My work colleagues were heading off to a strip club but I didn't want to go there. I wanted to stay with the gorgeous girl I had just met.

Girl X and I decided to try a place around the corner, a live music venue that was open a bit later. We got in and to our amusement there was an Elvis impersonator performing that night. Girl X and I really hit it off and got on really well and it was obvious we both fancied each other rotten. Even her accent made me go weak at the knees. After spending most of the night kissing and talking, with a bit of dancing thrown in, we went down to the local 'nightclub' to see if my flatmates or her friends were about so we could have a party back at mine.

As soon as we got there a huge fight broke out in the middle of the road outside the club, a really vicious scrap that had to be split up by Gardaí, the Irish police. We found everyone and we all went back to my house for that party. I had had such a brilliant night with Girl X that I was busy thinking how glad I was to have moved over here to this wonderful town with such lovely inhabitants.

The party back at my house was pretty loud and fun, but I got so drunk that I went upstairs and forgot Girl X was downstairs and ended up kissing my housemate's sister again. Then Girl X came upstairs as I was going to the toilet and when I saw her I wanted her, so I ended up kissing her again. Unsurprisingly I was caught red-handed, for this drunken misdemeanour I received a well-deserved punch in the face from both women, harder than any man to date had ever hit me. One of them called me an 'English bastard', which was a bit ill informed, but I got the message and stayed in my room the rest of the night.

I felt embarrassed and ashamed that I had behaved in such a way, I had thought that kind of behaviour had been abandoned in my early 20s. My two flatmates came upstairs to ask why the two ladies were so upset and I admitted what I had been doing, though thankfully they could see how plastered I was and were just relieved that that was all that had happened.

Next day, Sunday, I started getting text messages from both of them. The flatmate's sister letting me know how much I had hurt her while Girl X texted a more urgent message. She said her ex, some guy called Alan, was at her house drunk attacking her and could I come up. I had been thinking about her all morning but decided to wait and see what happened as I was in no fit state to go anywhere, let alone have a fight. In the end she texted later to say that she had got some friends or family to come up and get rid of him and that she was OK now. I was relieved at that, I don't like the thought of anyone being attacked, let alone a woman.

The next Monday at work, Girl X texted me a few times and it seemed she was willing to forgive my behaviour on the Saturday before. I was relieved, as I had really liked her. I dashed home from work that night and quickly showered and changed before getting a taxi up to her house in Woodvale Manor, just off a road named Tom Bellew Avenue.

My housemates had warned me not to go up to her house under any circumstances, but when I asked them why I shouldn't they wouldn't say, and in any case I really wanted to see her regardless of what they said. When I got there Girl X had made me dinner, which was a lovely thought even though I still felt rough from the weekend and couldn't eat much of it. We then sat in her living room and talked for a while before she asked me to stay the night, which I did. We had the most amazing evening ever. I remember thinking to myself, 'Your life's almost complete, son, you done the right thing moving over here.'

Girl X and I saw each other the next night and in fact every night for the next ten days, except one when I was too exhausted and just went to my bed after work. We got on brilliantly and the physical side of our relationship was amazing. On that Tuesday night she told me that she or her family were something to do with some paramilitary organisation. I had been warned about Dundalk when I told a mate Ricky at 3663 where I was going, he told me the town was 'staunchly Republican'. I didn't believe her when she told me this and frankly I didn't really care and didn't give it a second thought. I just wanted to be with her, I was falling rapidly in love and I think she was too. The only wee thing that niggled me about her was that she always asked if my housemate's sister had been in touch, every day. I couldn't blame her for being a little suspicious or jealous considering the way I had behaved the first time we met, so I chose just to reassure her. She made me happy at the time and I didn't want anything ruining that. I met some of her family, both at her house and at her mother's, and I found them to be very nice to me, especially her sister and brother-in-law.

A few days before Christmas we left her house to walk into town. A neighbour of her's stopped us in the street, a black guy who introduced himself as Sydney. Girl X and he had a brief conversation and they obviously knew each other, but this Sydney gave me a few funny looks before we went on our way. I later found out that he was a friend of another of Girl X's exes, named Junior, and that there had been some kind of hassle between them but I didn't ask what.

Chapter 16
Xmas Eve

I woke up on Christmas Eve morning in my girlfriend's house. We were both happy and decided to go into town. I had changed my plans for Christmas Day and was now going to spend it with her at her house. We walked hand in hand into the town centre. We went into the shopping centre and, while she was in buying something, I felt a sudden compulsion. I raced into the florist and bought a lovely red rose, which I presented to her outside. She went bright red and smiled at me. We then decided to head off for a couple of drinks as it was Christmas Eve. I was looking forward to a quiet Christmas with her and maybe a party with the lads on Boxing Day, or St Stephen's Day as it's known over there.

The first pub we tried was Harvey's in Park Street. They refused to serve us point blank. I've no idea why as we were both well dressed and weren't drunk, and I had never been in the place before in my life. This wasn't the last strange thing to happen that day. We hung around town for a bit then went to a pub called Brady's. After a couple in there I told her I was going back to my old house in Demense to see if I had any letters and to ask if they had found my ID card that I had obtained from the Gardaí only a few weeks before and had mysteriously lost. My landlord at Demense hadn't been happy at me leaving to move in with the lads at short notice, but I had let him keep half my deposit in lieu of notice so he wasn't put out of pocket and he had eventually been OK about it.

I got to my old house and asked if I had any mail, and was pleasantly surprised to find a card and a letter from my dad. To my relief, there was a cheque inside for one hundred pounds which meant I would have enough money to have a nice Christmas now. I stuffed the letter, card and cheque into my pocket and headed back towards the pub and my girlfriend, then I realised I hadn't got her a Christmas present. I stopped into a card shop and then went into a chemist's and bought her a bottle of Yves St Laurent perfume in a trendy blue bottle. She seemed a little surprised when I told her I loved her and gave her the card and present, but she looked happy too. I couldn't have been happier. Every pub we went into that night had music television and the song 'Feel' by Robbie Williams seemed to be on a constant loop, playing everywhere we went. I had hated the song when I first heard it but now I really liked it. It was a good song and it filled me with hope and made me smile. Then things started to go wrong.

Several incidents that I thought nothing of at the time occurred which to this day still can't be explained properly. When we were in a Park Street pub, my girlfriend's ex, Alan, walked in, saw us together, then left. Very strange. We tried to get into the Train pub again, downstairs, but as soon as we walked in I was grabbed by a barman and literally thrown out of the pub doors, straight towards the bouncers, an obvious ploy to tempt the bouncers into beating me up, but thankfully they let me through as I kept my head down. I didn't get it. I knew Mr McGlynn who owned the Gaelic bar also owned the Train and I was aware that my friends and I had been a bit loud in there a few weeks previously at the Celtic v Blackburn game and had been asked to leave, but that had all been good natured banter and I had been into the Train since to apologise and they had accepted my apology. The only thing I can think of that might have caused me being thrown out was the fact that there was still no sign of Mick. Maybe he had upset someone and done a runner and because I was Scottish they thought I was something to do with it all, but I most certainly wasn't.

My girlfriend wasn't very happy with this but we made our way to another kind of restaurant/bar around the corner. Then her phone started to ring. Apparently one or more of her uncles had been in the pub we had just been kicked out of and wanted to know what it was all about. She changed completely after this phone call and seemed a bit distant. I wondered what on earth was going on.

We later went to McManus's pub, which was closing early as it was of course Christmas Eve. The pub had musicians playing; indeed that is where the world famous Corrs first played publicly I think, as they are from Dundalk. My girlfriend took a few more calls and we had a pint together, then the band started to play the Irish national anthem. Everyone stood up for this, but as I recognised this song as a Celtic song and I was Scottish and a little tipsy I didn't stand. I was threatened by some little rat but I steadfastly refused to stand for any national anthem other than my own, and some other people told this rat to leave me alone and as he obviously didn't fancy his chances alone he backed off. Not before threatening me though, but I didn't pay much attention. Ironically I felt more Scottish than ever when I lived over there.

The two of us went back to Brady's where my girlfriend got talking to some people, and after a while she started to ignore me. She had completely changed her attitude to me since we had been kicked out of the Train, I've no idea why, maybe it was embarrassment. After a while I got sick of her ignoring me in favour of the guy she was talking too and just walked out, intent on going home to my bed as I was exhausted, it had been a heavy week at work after all and I didn't want an argument. She did come after me, but I wasn't convinced and just kept walking away to get a taxi back to my place. To be honest I was just as upset about not seeing my friends and family from Scotland as I was at how the evening had panned out after it had started so well. I got a taxi back to mine where there was a party going on. I wasn't in much of a party mood and went upstairs alone to lie on my bed and hopefully get some sleep.

Digressing slightly for a moment, on the 16 December my mother in Scotland had a dream that I had been killed in a fire that someone had started deliberately. She told one of her friends the next day. Her friend will no longer discuss this premonition with anyone.

Chapter 17
The Nightmare

Later that evening I started getting intimate text messages from my girlfriend, apologising and asking me to go up to her house. I wanted to sort it all out, but I had a nagging doubt that I should leave it until the morning, especially after what she told me her or her family might be involved in. The rest of the evening and indeed the next two months are all like one giant cartoon, but I assure you it is no laughing matter.

Only one of my housemate's friends who were present had a car and he was drunk. However, everyone seems to drink drive over there and I convinced him to take me up to her house and the lads came with us. When we got there I noticed that my girlfriend appeared pleased to see me, but also that the guy she had been talking to in the pub was there, and he was tooled up big time, with what looked like a pickaxe handle. When we walked in, my housemate, who's sister I had been kissing before I had started seeing my girlfriend, joked to my girlfriend that I had been with his sister down at our house before we came up, which of course I hadn't. Her eyes turned from her usual loving look to an evil stare that I will never forget, and she picked up a plastic mop and attacked me with it, knocking me to the ground, though I managed to protect my face and head. It took my housemate to tell her that it was all a joke to get her to stop. She calmed down but was still acting strangely.

We all went to the living room where everybody continued drinking. Apparently the guy from the pub had come home with my girl as she had received a text message from her coloured neighbour Sydney telling her that someone was trying to break in.

The guy from the pub looked a right scumbag and didn't look in the least bit pleased to see me.

I have my suspicions why. My girlfriend gave me my Christmas presents, which included a lovely blue shirt, but there was a strange atmosphere in the house. Everybody was absolutely plastered. There is no other word for it. Highly intoxicated. The scumbag from the pub was obviously itching to give someone a right beating and I got the impression it was me he wanted a fight with, but the lads got pissed off at his aggression and for the time being he shut up and had his weapon temporarily taken off him.

This is where the cartoon starts. The drink was running out and I went to sleep. When I woke up there was no one in the house except me and two, possibly three people. I know they had a car outside as I now remember seeing the headlights. There was no sign of my housemates. I used to think this was a robbery but I see now that it wasn't, there was nothing in that house worth stealing. Two guys battered me absolutely senseless for no reason, though there may have been a third individual present. They knew what they were doing all right. I had no chance on my own. The last thing I remember is being cracked on the head with what I think was the pickaxe handle and seeing a white flash of light. They didn't stop there. I was dumped on the sofa, robbed of my mobile phone, jacket and the cheque from my dad that I had foolishly been earlier brandishing. These items were never recovered. It gets worse.

The house was then set on fire, as my attackers obviously thought I was dead and were keen to hide this dreadful deed in an inferno. They jammed the front door shut so that I would be unable to escape the flames, even if I did regain consciousness. The smoke alarm was either sabotaged or didn't work. The sofa I was dumped on was non fire-retardant, against EU law, and would have gone up like a bail of hay. And so my life was coming to an end, what had become a dream move had turned into the darkest of nightmares. I was beaten unconscious, trapped and I was going to be burned to death. And it was all for no reason. Ian Colquhoun was going to die.

Chapter 18
Coma

What the fuck is happening? Where am I? It looks like I'm in a house in Mid Calder, near Livingston. It's so horrible in here. So dark. I'm so afraid. What's going on? It's dark outside and inside. It smells too, oh what a ghastly smell. I'm not alone. Maybe one of these people in the house with me knows where I am. They don't say much. They all look pretty out of it. Hang on, I'll check in the next room. Fuck me it's hard to walk. I can barely get two yards. Here, I know some of the people in this house. This can't be right. Some of these people are my school friends, but some of them died years ago.

Where am I? What's happening? Why is no one talking? I'm kind of hungry but I need to get out of here. It's like some kind of horrible waiting room. I'm so hungry, what's that there? Looks like fish and chips, that'll do. I open it. The paper is full of shit and maggots. Jesus, I don't like it in here. If I hang around in here any longer I think I'm going to die. How do I escape though, I can hardly walk. No one else seems to want out of this place.

Hang on, what's that out there? In the distance there's what looks like an old-fashioned steam engine coming towards the house. It has a huge bright lamp on the end with a brilliant shining light. The light is so compelling. I want to go towards it. The light makes me feel safe. I can hardly walk though. What if I miss the train? I need to get outside to the light and away from this miserable place. The light will look after me. I'm so afraid, so terribly afraid. I'm trying to get down the steps and out of this horrid house as quickly as I can. I need to get to the light. Some unknown force is stopping me from getting to it though. The light is getting closer, oh please, God, let me go to the light and end this nightmare. It's here, the light is here, but I can't get to it. The train is outside, waiting for me, its bright light illuminating the outside of the house. It's no use, I can't get to it, it's started to move off, NO, NO PLEASE WAIT, NOOOOOOOOOOOOOOOOO!

Now what is going on? I'm being loaded on to a plane, looks a bit like a jet fighter. I'm lying down. It's really big and spacious inside. We're flying. There are a few nurses in the back of the plane with me. What's going on? What happened to the train? Why am I not in the horrible house anymore? Hang on a minute, what are these nurses doing? NOOOOO WHAT THE FUCK ARE YOU DOING? STOP IT! They're chopping off my legs. NOOOOOO! Please, don't do that, I need them. I won't be able to go to work without them. No, please don't. Don't cut them off. Oh my God. They've chopped off my legs. Now what are they doing? Oh God, this is sick. They've chopped off my legs and thrown them out of the back of the plane! Bastards! I didn't say you could do that. Oh nooooooooooooo.

Ah! This is more like it. I'm in Tokyo now, driving what looks like a giant fairground dodgem car. The bright lights and all the noise is reassuring, though curiously there is no traffic on the roads whatsoever, only me in my dodgem car. I've got passengers too. A couple of guys in suits and four beautiful women. I'm zooming around Tokyo. Funny, I don't remember ever planning to come here. What is going on? There's music that seems to be blasting right across the city via a citywide PA system. I recognise some of the songs. Oh my God, it's 'Kung Fu Fighting' by Bus Stop. Haa mooo chaaaa. There are so many nightclubs here, in fact, almost every building is a nightclub. But I'm loving this driving around in my giant dodgem car with my cool passengers. We zoom around for what seems like days but at the same time it feels like only a few moments.

We stop outside a club with big bouncers on the door. We approach, it sounds like there's an absolutely wicked party going on inside the club. My passengers get in but when I try to enter, the bouncer puts his arm out. He knows my name. 'Sorry, Ian, not tonight, pal.' I argue with him, complaining that he's just let my passengers in but he answers, 'I'm sorry, Ian, it's not your time. Not tonight. You've got a lot of unfinished business to attend too.'

Exasperated at not being allowed in, I try the club next door. Again it's, 'Sorry Ian, not tonight, it's not your time.' I'm getting pissed off at this. This is happening at every club. There sounds like an awesome party inside but although the bouncers say I'm not barred, they say it isn't my time, that I have unfinished business to attend too, that I'm not to worry, I'll be allowed in when it's my time. None of these fabulous sounding and looking clubs let me in. I return to my dodgem car and start to drive around Tokyo again. 'Kung Fu Fighting' is on a loop now and is really starting to get on my nerves. I drive around the city alone, it still feels good, but why won't they let me in anywhere?

Now I'm driving a shitty MK II Ford Escort. It looks like the desert I'm driving through. It's just one big long single-track road ahead and it's absolutely straight. I can't even drive a manual but I seem to be managing this one OK. The car is dark blue. I just seem to be driving aimlessly towards a far horizon that never seems to get any closer. There are no objects in the landscape with which I could judge how far I've driven, but it's been bloody hundreds of miles anyway. Hang on, what's that up ahead? A bus stop? Out here? There's someone in it too. I think I'll stop and ask them where I am and, more importantly, where I'm going. I pull in and stop in the bus stop.

It's Shelley, my girlfriend from over two years ago. Not knowing what to say but so pleased to see her, I offer her a lift and she nods and gets into the passenger seat. 'It's so good to see you,' I say to her. 'I'm so sorry I fucked things up.' She doesn't say anything at first and we just continue driving. 'This is weird, Shelley. I'm scared, what's happening?' I ask. She answers 'Listen to me, Ian. It's going to be hard but you're going to be OK. You're going to have to fight though.' This scares me but I somehow know what she's talking about. She looks so beautiful. We talk for a while whilst I drive until we come to what looks like a stone cottage at the side of the road where she asks me to stop the car. She gets out. 'Don't go, please don't go,' I ask, but she answers, 'I can't come with you, Ian. You're going to be OK, but it's going to be tough and you're going to have to fight. Everything is going to be alright, Ian.' Understanding and now with a courageous heart after this conversation I drive away, a little less terrified than I had been for the last while. But the road seems endless, I drive on and on and on...

Ah, this seems more familiar. I'm in the queue for the Liquid Room in Edinburgh. I seem to be the only one in the queue except my friends, who are human. The rest are weird, kind of like chickens but with humanoid bipedal legs and, instead of the little bit under the neck that most chickens have, they have what look like clear plastic bags full of clear liquid. They're very scary but I don't know why. I walk down the steep steps into the club but am horrified when I see what's inside. There's a huge talking television booming random questions at me. It's black. Hold on. It's wearing a Hibs scarf. The big telly that's shouting questions at me is a Hibby! I shout back at it, 'WE ARE HIBERNIAN FC, WE HATE JAM TARTS AND WE HATE DUNDEE, WE WILL FIGHT WHEREVER WE MAY BE FOR WE ARE THE MENTAL H.F.C.' The telly responds by roaring 'Glory Glory to the Hibees' back at me. Who would have thought it eh, a Hibby telly. And a huge one at that. It's roaring random questions at me but I'm not listening anymore…

Wahey, this is more like it. I'm at a house party now, and I'm the only guy. There are loads of women in the room, I think they said they were all nurses, but they certainly don't look like nurses. One's really sexy. In fact they all are, but this one's pretty stunning. Black hair and wearing stockings and suspenders, leaning over me. Her name is Jennifer. Doesn't get much better than being in a room full of scantily clad women. It's weird though, every few hours one load of them disappear and another load take their place. It's almost as if they're working shifts just to be around me. I must be doing something right to be getting all this attention. Oh no not again…

Right, this is getting silly now. I think I'm in hospital, but I can see out of the window. I'm in Almondbank Primary School in Livingston. Why am I being cared for here? What has happened? Hold on, there's a nurse blabbering to me. She says, 'Ian, do you know where you are yet?' 'Yes,' I reply. 'Where are you then?' she continued. 'I'm in Almondbank primary school in Craigshill, Livingston and the milk has just been delivered.' The nurse seems more than a little pissed off at this reply and continues, 'No, no, no!'

I have tried, before now, to deliver what you have just read in italics in several idioms, but have never been able to describe what was going on in such a way that is universally understandable to everyone. It is for that reason that I wrote down my experience of being in a seven-week coma just as I saw it. To this day my experiences in the coma still affect me and I will never forget the strange things that I saw, heard and did while I was 'in limbo', between life and death as it were. That's what I saw. I know it was a mix of dreams, trauma and reactions to my surroundings and the events taking place around me as I fought for my life, but there was something else, something religious and supernatural, almost a view to the other side. You may not choose to believe this, you may have your own preconceptions about life and death, but I assure you these 'dreams' were not just in my imagination. If you choose to believe your own preconceptions over the testimony of a dying man, and dying I most certainly was, and disregard the above as rubbish then you have my deepest sympathy. Only someone who has been in a similar position is qualified to make judgements about what happened to my mind and soul in that coma, though I will now try and explain things a bit more clearly.

The horrible house and train and bright light part, that is the bit that still terrifies me to this day. It was awful. I had heard about people seeing a bright light when they are about to die, and although at the time I thought I just wanted to get on the train and get away, I see now that that was around one of the three times I was given the Catholic last rites and resuscitated. Some old school friends of mine who died were in that house with me, as well as some people I know, who to the best of my knowledge are still alive.

The plane thing is easier to explain. The motion of being wheeled through to the operating theatre may have caused me to feel like I was flying, but although I was under anaesthetic when my burned right through legs were amputated, I swear I was still well aware of what was going on. The nurses throwing my legs out of the airlock was purely symbolic I think, but I recognised one of the nurses who was present at my amputations, which makes it a strange 'episode' indeed.

The Tokyo episode is somewhat bizarre as well. The Bus Stop song 'Kung Fu Fighting' had indeed been a comedy favourite party anthem of my friends and I in 1998, and we had all got sick of it, just like in my vision. Quite where Tokyo or the giant fairground dodgem car came from is anyone's guess, but I think being knocked back from all those fabulous nightclubs and being told it wasn't my time yet meant that it simply wasn't my time to die. I still believe that I have an as yet unfulfilled purpose in life and that is partly why I didn't die, despite the overwhelming odds stacked against me. I think the nightclubs were my trauma-laden soul's vision of heaven.

As for seeing my old girlfriend in one of these visions, well, I can't explain that one. However, that particular experience, or vision, call it what you like, gave my soul and life force the courage and the will to battle on and fight for my life, no matter what it took. It was also the first one of my 'visions' that didn't have any kind of sinister aspect to it. I still think about her lots.

The one with the talking television and the chicken people is a little easier to explain and obviously happened as I began to regain consciousness, though when you wake from a coma like that you are often delirious and hallucinate, thanks to all the painkillers and other drugs you are given. These drugs also induce temporary amnesia. The Hibs supporting television was a real TV in my room that my visitors had draped a Hibernian FC scarf over, and the questions I was hearing would have been nurses or visitors trying to ascertain what degree of consciousness I had reached. The chicken things under the throats were me seeing my drip bags and confusing them with being real creatures, thanks to all the morphine and other drugs. My mum's friend's daughter had sent me over a tape of Hibs songs and it had obviously been played to me while I was 'out of it'.

The thing about being at a party with the nurses was a bit embarrassing but they later assured me that they had heard this sort of thing from patients in similar circumstances lots of times before. I did have a room full of nurses, and Jennifer was gorgeous, but she certainly wasn't going around dressed in sexy lingerie and neither were any of the other members of the brilliant team who kept me alive. That was a product again of the drugs they had pumped me into me. When I started to wake up, I remember arguing with one of the better-looking nurses. I was convinced that I had been living with her in Dublin and that we were sleeping together, and I believed it too and must have seemed genuinely upset when the nurse in question giggled and tried to put me straight.

Thinking I was in Almondbank Primary School was the last one, but it's curious as I didn't even attend that school as a boy. I must have been almost at full consciousness at this point, but not quite, as the nurse seemed genuinely frustrated at my answer. The view outside my window looked like the back of the aforementioned school though, and I probably heard the tea and coffee trolley on the ward and that would have made me think the milk was being delivered.

So how did I get from being attacked for no reason and left for dead, locked in a burning house, to waking up from a seven-week coma? Well, here goes...

Chapter 19
Attempted Murder

Someone in Woodvale Manor had heard the disturbance and called the Gardaí and a fire engine was soon on its way. I owe my life to a brave Garda officer named Aidan Lyons. This man got me out of the death trap that those cowardly scumbags had left me in. As the front door had been jammed he had to break it down before pulling me from the inferno, and I think he burned himself in the process. Thankfully I have absolutely no recollection of the fire or being burned, partly due to the beating I received and partly because the non-fire-retardant sofa fumes and flame smoke had knocked me out. I apparently had regained consciousness just before being rescued as I had managed to crawl into the hall, but as the door was sabotaged I would have been trapped. One of the scumbags involved in my attack was apprehended at the scene but for some strange reason wasn't arrested.

I don't know where everyone else from the party had gone as I had fallen asleep. Girl X later told me that they had all gone to my house to rectify the no alcohol situation, leaving the pickaxe wielding nutter and me alone in the house. If this is the case, how did he get out of the house? I wish I could remember more details.

From the house I was taken by ambulance to the local hospital, the Louth, but they quickly decided that I was far too critical to be treated there so I was to be transferred to Ireland's dedicated burns unit in St James's Hospital, Dublin. I was of course unconscious during all this and would be for some time. So while kids around the world were opening Christmas presents, I was a swollen, blistered, charred wreck in the back of an ambulance fighting for my life. I was brought into ITU. On admission to hospital my injuries were as follows:

A gaping head wound consistent with assault.
Lungs full of black fluid from the smoke.
Kidney failure – from smoke inhalation.
A singed foreskin (no laughing).

Burnt

Heart problems.
65% burns.

The burns were to my chest/abdomen, arms, hands, chin and, worst of all, my legs. My legs were burned right through, even to the bone. They were going to have to come off if I was to live.

My mum, still troubled by that dream she had about me being the victim of arson that she had on 16 December, got the news from a policeman on Christmas morning. She phoned the hospital in panic and was told that I was going to die and that she had better hurry if she wanted to see me. My distraught sister and her friend, Suzanne, and my mum knew that my dad had to be told what had happened to me. Suzanne drove and Angela, who like me and my mum hadn't seen my dad in over ten years now, found they had to drive to his house on Christmas morning to give him and his new wife the 'good' news. It must have been awful for everyone concerned. Angela was the one to break the news to him.

It's hard enough getting a same day flight most of the time but imagine trying to get one on Christmas Day. And imagine the stress my family were under, being thrown back into the mix again after so long and under such dire circumstances.

Chapter 20
Here Comes The Cavalry

My mum and Angela arrived in Dublin on Boxing Day. Up until then only my girlfriend had been at my side and I don't envy her having had to sit and look at me in my burned, severely blistered state with all kinds of life support machines bleeping and hissing for hours on end. My mum and Angela got a taxi from the airport and the driver was playing the radio when he picked them up. I had been all over Irish TV and radio news since it had happened, though as I was out of it no one knew anything about the incident. When the driver heard their Scottish accents and where they wanted to go (St James's) he instinctively turned off the songs on the radio. He knew who they were.

My dad and his new wife Susan arrived later that evening. My mum and Angela initially stayed in a convent and at the hospital, before they were sorted out through family connections with digs in Dublin with a kind man named Morris, while my dad and his wife eventually stayed in a little B&B. There was understandably and obviously tension between them all at the hospital, but that is none of my business. My mum's friend Jeanette and my friends Davie, Tony and Jenny made it over to see me while they still could. At first my friends were told to go home because I was surely going to die. My friends and my mum and sister were both soon suspicious of my girlfriend's role in what had happened to me, whatever their reasons, and soon she was stopped from seeing me. The medical staff continually asked all of my visitors if they knew where I had got the nasty head wound from. When I myself asked the nurses what it was they went all quiet and just told me not to worry about it and that it wasn't a burn. I still have the scar today.

My mum and co had to sign forms allowing the surgeons to amputate my now useless legs to save me from gangrene and death, and on 28 December 2002 I had my right leg amputated halfway between the knee and the ankle and my left leg amputated just above the knee. My folks were told that it still might not be enough to save my life, and all in all I had fourteen operations while I was in St James, most when I was in the coma and a few when I regained consciousness.

During this time the support from the hospital chaplaincy and my mum's own parish in Craigshill was absolutely immense. They gave my mum and sister money to live on, as Dublin can be expensive, and they organised massed prayers for my life. Not only were people in the hospital chapel and St Andrew's Chapel in Craigshill praying for me, but thanks to the Internet there were thousands of people praying for my life all over the world, from as far away as Papua New Guinea. I know this praying helped save me and brought me back from the brink.

Those seven weeks I was out cold must have been a living hell for my friends and family, all that waiting and uncertainty coupled with having been fragmented as a family for so long. My parents and Angela were taken aside three times and told that I would probably be dead in ten minutes. I was given the last rites three times. Yet somehow my burned broken body and soul fought on. I think part of why I fought so hard was because of the injustice of what had happened to me. I've never seen myself as being a strong person, but this incident made a lot of people say that I am. Those seven weeks of the coma were a nightmare for my family and friends, and I'd imagine for those angels, and no word suits them better, the nurses who looked after me. But for me the real nightmare began when I regained full consciousness.

At the font, my Christening

Starting out, a wee bundle

Me in my Hibs jumper

Hibs player in the making?

I was always happy

Sometimes deep in thought

A young historian in the making

Auntie Kath, Gran, Mum and me

Me and a drink in 1996   **Fooling about in 1998**

Above and below, the Buckfast days are long gone

Burnt

Dundalk, this is where I was left for dead

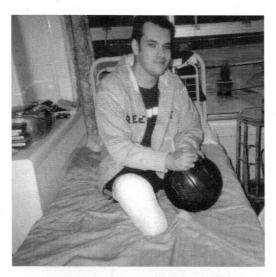

2003, in hospital, over the worst

2003, in my ward room at Astley Anslie

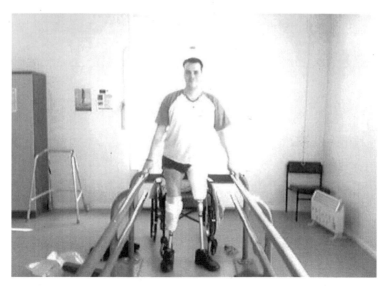

2005, learning to walk again

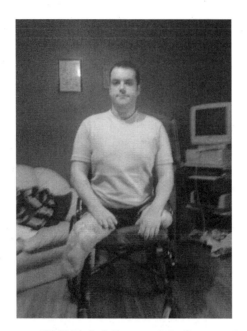

Well healed, just need the legs

Men In White pimped my legs

Me with mad scientists from the TV show *Men In White*

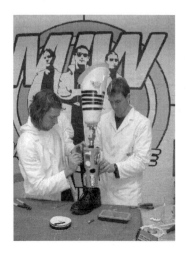

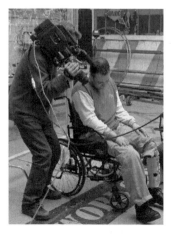

Having my leg pimped up

On the set of *Men In White*

**Acting it up, me made up on the film set of Brook
Lapping Productions for the film 'Ocean Of Fear'**

Me at home, a rare leg occasion

As I am today

My beloved Hibs, my stand

Chapter 21
Wakey, Wakey

I remember it was left to my mum to tell me what had happened. I was told I had been in a fire, and that I had almost died, but that I was going to live now. I was also told about my legs. I remember dismissing this at first as I had what I now know is phantom limb pain, and could still feel my feet. I could even feel my Nike trainers. Then I looked down. I was so weak and skinny from being drip-fed and from lying down for two months that it was an effort merely to move, but I looked down and, sure enough, half my legs were missing. Shit! The rest of me was wrapped up in bandages and dressings of all sorts. At first I deluded myself that this was a dream. Any minute now I was going to wake up in my bed and get up for work. Any minute now. Any minute now.

I started to cry, wailing uncontrollably like a child and saying 'no, no, no, this can't be happening.' I as yet had absolutely no recollection of the attack in Dundalk. My mum and sister reassured me that I wasn't to worry and that they thought I was amazing. I didn't. I couldn't believe what was happening to me. That was me fucked. Life over. I couldn't even speak properly as I had been given a tracheotomy to help me to breathe. I could barely move. All I could do was cry.

At first I blamed my family for allowing my legs to be amputated, though it did soon sink in the more I got my wits back they had had no choice. Initially I resented being kept alive in this now severely disabled state. I thought I would have been better off not being pulled from the flames at all. For a couple of days after regaining consciousness all I wanted to do was take my own life. But that was utterly impossible, firstly as I could hardly move and secondly because I was watched almost 24 hours a day.

The suicidal feelings didn't last long though. Partly through encouragement from friends, family and medical staff and partly from my own resolve, I realised it was decision time. I'd already had a couple of days crying in my bed and didn't fancy that for the rest of my life, so I decided just to get on with it, though I was still terrified about the future.

I remember asking for a set of crutches so that I could go home, with hindsight a funny request as I had no legs but at the time I thought I could just get up and leave. I was given a wheelchair but initially wouldn't go near the thing. That was just too much. I knew nothing of prosthetics and thought they would issue me with a pair of prosthetic legs within a few days. I didn't know about waiting for my wounds to heal or taking into account the fact that I needed several more operations before I could even think about getting fitted for new limbs. However, once the consultant told me that I would be getting new legs, eventually that gave me something to aim for.

Soon after I had 'woken up' as it were, I had checked my genitals to see if they were burned away. To my relief they weren't burned, save for a small singe to my foreskin and simple circumcision easily solved this problem. If they had been burnt I really would have killed myself, but they weren't, though in my mental state at the time I didn't think any woman would want to go near this charred, scarred half a man ever again. It had been a close thing where that was concerned though, the burns on my legs stop at the top a mere two inches from my genitals, and one surgeon thinks that I had probably pissed myself during the fire and that would have saved them.

As I mentioned before, I had fourteen operations in St James's. I don't remember most of them as I was out of it, but I remember getting my right hand done and getting what was left of my legs skin grafted. My right hand prior to this operation was horrid, all bandaged up with a big swollen unbendable thumb and the end digits looked like burned matchsticks rather than fingers. I had a catheter bag inserted into my penis after my legs were grafted to stop me from urinating on the graft sites and poisoning them. The hand operation was successful, they managed to bend the unburned portions of the digits back onto the lower digits to give me four stubby little fingers that were extremely painful at the time and I didn't think I'd ever be able to move them.

Seeing my dad again wasn't as weird as I thought it might have been, in fact it was like he had never been away. Well that's families for you!

Chapter 22
A Fighting Chance

I still had some serious surgery to get through. My chest and stomach were covered in a thick black crust that looked and smelled ghastly and reminded me of a turtle's shell, while on my right leg below my one remaining knee there was a gaping hole with exposed bone that needed major patching up.

Despite my injuries I was greatly encouraged by the invaluable support I received from my family, friends and brilliant hospital staff. A few days after I got over my little suicidal spell I was able to crack jokes, which even surprised me considering the right state I was in. The most annoying thing after waking up wasn't the strange sense of fear I had that my attackers were coming to finish me off, it was the fact that I wasn't allowed anything to drink because of my tracheotomy. It wasn't for want of asking, I can tell you.

I remember asking one nurse for a drink of water, to which she replied 'No sorry, Ian.'

I replied, 'Milk?'

'No.'

'Cola?'

'No.'

'Irn Bru?'

'No.'

'Coffee?'

'No.'

This went on for days, I didn't give up asking but they didn't relent and they were, of course, doing me a favour as the liquid might have choked me because of my tracheotomy. I must have asked for every non-alcoholic drink known to mankind. I did manage to sneak a drink of Tizer that someone had bought me one night though when no one was looking. It had been placed about a yard from me on the window ledge, but a yard to me in that physical state was like a mile. It took me half an hour to grab it. It tasted so good and quenched my maddening thirst. Of course, I wasn't dehydrated; I was being fed through one of those ghastly tubes they put up your nose and into your stomach, which was extremely uncomfortable.

Burnt

Nighttime was the worst in St James's. Daytime flew by as I had agonising dressing changes in the morning and sometimes a bath, then I had my mum and sister come in to see me, and sometimes sister Maureen, a nun who had come all the way from Livingston just to visit me and support my mum. In the afternoon I would have the physiotherapist or the psychologist in. The physio was nice but I largely ignored her as I didn't see at the time what good doing exercises in bed would do me. The psychologist was a different kettle of fish. I just told him what he wanted to hear, or rather what I thought he wanted to hear, that I was OK and that I was coping OK.

Nighttime was a different matter altogether. Around 8pm my visitors would have to go home and I was left with the TV, which thankfully had MTV. I remember watching an old favourite of mine, the film Zulu, but I had to turn it off at the scene where the hospital gets set on fire.

I also remember the first time I realised that my penis was in full working order after its circumcision. I had agonisingly had the catheter removed earlier that day and was lying alone at night watching MTV when a video came on. It was 'All the Things She Said' by T.A.T.U and any red blooded male who's seen this video will understand how it made me realise that everything was in full working order, if you know what I mean.

The next two videos were 'Beautiful' by Christina Aguilera and 'Come Undone' by Robbie Williams. The lyrics to both these songs had a positive effect on me, for different reasons, though I had to turn the Robbie one off as it reminded me of his previous hit 'Feel' which had been playing in all the pubs on Christmas Eve.

MTV asides though, I hated the nights in St James's. My attention span was badly affected from the coma so I couldn't concentrate on the TV for long, and sitting up to read would have been uncomfortable. Nighttime was when I did my planning for the future, my thinking, and when I dwelled a little on what had happened to me in that town I had loved so much.

By now I had no contact with my girlfriend, but to be honest I had more important stuff like having no legs and what was going to happen to me to worry about. My family, friends, doctors and I all agreed that it was best for me to go back to Scotland, back to the burns unit at St John's Hospital in Livingston to have the rest of my surgery and begin my rehabilitation. My medical expenses had been covered by a reciprocal agreement between the Republic and Britain, but rehab was impossibly expensive over there and, in any case, I needed to be near my friends and family now.

Chapter 23
Fuck's Sake Hibs

When I was well enough to sit up and read, I read the dozens upon dozens of get well cards I had been sent, but I got more bad news of a different sort when I opened a package from my uncle Ron in Edinburgh. It contained a newspaper cutting from the Evening News with a match report on the New Year derby between Hibs and Hearts at Tynecastle. It had finished 4-4, but Hibs had thrown away a two-goal lead in injury time, meaning it was just like a defeat. For a minute I was more upset about that than about losing my bloody legs! Not for long though, as it showed me that nothing much had changed as far as my beloved team were concerned back home, and I knew now that I would at least be able to go and see them again, so in the end the article actually cheered me up!

By now I had got over my wheelchair phobia and was letting my mum and sister wheel me down to the hospital café for coffee every day, though I was still too weak to push it myself, and my right hand and my new 'stubby' fingers were still very sore.

My mum knew for sure then that I had no lasting damage to my brain, as when she wheeled me down to the café one afternoon I asked her for some money to phone Davie. I dialled the number, including the full international dialling code, correctly and without consulting any kind of diary.

My dad was working so he came over at the weekends to see me. I was visited in hospital too by Neil and some of the great lads I used to work with. They had a benefit night for me and a football tournament to raise money so that my mum and sister could stay in Dublin with me, my old team-mates competing for the 'Jockser' cup, which they presented to me and which I still have. I still had phantom limb pain, that feeling that your feet are still there, and I still suffer from it to this day, though nowhere near as bad as I did at first. The thing with phantom limb pain is that your brain always thinks that you have four limbs, no matter what happens, and it's a process of taking a combination of anti epilepsy drugs and painkillers along with psychologically adjusting to your limb loss that helps control it, at least that's what has worked for me.

It had been barely two months since the fire but already things were looking encouraging to me. I was eager to get home, particularly when I found out that my silly breach of the peace charge had been dropped and that as I wasn't working the debt people couldn't really touch me anymore. I got a card on Valentine's Day, hand delivered, obviously from the nurses on the ward, but that perked me up. I had also been allowed to eat and drink again for a little while, and to celebrate this my lovely American nurse, Maureen, had bought me a pizza, which is still the nicest thing I have ever eaten. I still had a long way to go but had done remarkably well since the attempt on my life and becoming severely disabled. I would be able to see all my friends once I was back in Scotland, too. But more importantly, I would be safe there. My sister and mum would no doubt be glad to see the back of Dublin, too.

Chapter 24
Back To Scotland

As I was still a stretcher case covered in dressings, I needed a special plane to fly me back to Edinburgh. The ward arranged for the Irish Air Force to fly me back on a transport plane, and on 18 February 2003 I was flown back to Scotland in a crude military plane. The crew were nice and even made us tea and coffee. All the staff that looked after me from when I was admitted to when I was transferred back to Scotland were highly skilled, highly professional and, just as importantly, always had a smile for me. They did a fantastic job of saving my life and putting me back together again. They were very supportive to my family, as was the generous hospital chaplaincy, and they couldn't have done a better job. If only the same could be said of Ireland's 'police' force…

The investigation into my attempted murder was a complete cock up from day one. Though the brave Garda who saved me from the inferno apprehended a scumbag at the scene, nothing further was done as far as I know. Obviously they assumed it was an accident, either that or they just didn't care. My mum had to approach them when she was staying in Dublin to get them to look at what had happened.

The Gardaí that Christmas morning took no forensic evidence; in fact no forensic examination took place until a full two weeks after, and only after my mum had asked them too. Plenty of time for any evidence to be removed, tampered with or just plain and simply contaminated by virtue of the passage of time. No doubt those who were on the scene that Christmas morning were keen to put it all down to an accident so they could get off for their Christmas dinner. When they finally did get around to doing a forensic examination all they concluded was that no accelerants (e.g. petrol) had been used, though the Gardaí did tell us about the door being jammed from the outside, about blood all over one of the inside doors and about the faulty/sabotaged smoke alarm and the death trap illegal sofa.

Burnt

Curiously, my then girlfriend later told me that all the mirrors had been stolen from the house, but long after we had split up I found a picture on the Internet of the room, taken after I was attacked, with a big mirror on the wall in the fire gutted room. We also found out that the house was the responsibility of North Eastern Health Board and my girlfriend was living in supported accommodation there, as she had been unwell for a number of years, which wasn't her fault. This should have meant that either way I would get compensation for my horrific injuries, if not via criminal injuries then via a civil claim against the health board over the sofa and smoke alarm. At the moment though that wasn't important.

Chapter 25
St John's

So on 18 February I was flown back to Edinburgh Turnhouse, where I was picked up by an ambulance with two nurses and taken to the burns unit at St John's Hospital in Livingston. I was given a huge room, and to my relief I had television. I was back in my hometown and couldn't wait for my friends to visit me. I was also very happy that my family had been spared all the hassle that went with me being in Dublin.

For the first time since that Christmas Eve in Dundalk I felt safe. Later I found out that there had been a patient on my Dublin ward from Cork whom had been the victim of a similar crime, but that his assailants had come back to the hospital to finish him off, unsuccessfully.

Now all I had to worry about was a lifetime of disability and the more immediate problems of my impending surgery and rehabilitation. I was home now.

Next day brought more bad news. On top of my horrendous injuries, I had become infected with a rare Asian strain of the MRSA super bug, apparently picked up in Dublin as there had been a victim of the horrific Bali bombing being treated there. The infection itself did little to me other than slow down the healing of my wounds, but the infection was an enormous risk to other patients, particularly the elderly. For this reason I was to be barrier nursed for the time being. Barrier nursing is essentially a loose form of quarantine. The nice room I was in had two sets of doors into it, with a wash hand basin unit in the alcove between the two doors. Anyone coming in to see me had to wash their hands and put on an apron, to minimise the risk of passing the nasty bug on to anyone.

I was still mostly covered in dressings, and of course still needed the 'tortoise shell' on my chest and abdomen removed and grafted, as well as major reconstructive surgery to my one remaining knee. It was actually pretty cool what the surgeons in Dublin had done to save that knee. It was now basically an artificial knee but made wholly of what was left of my right leg. It's basically a moving knee but with my old calf muscle bunched up and grafted around the side to give me plenty of cushioning. However, the bit below it was what now required the surgery to cover the gaping hole, and the exposed bone of my patella (knee cap) also had a hole in the flesh meaning that I could see my kneecap moving around when it wasn't dressed. My back was still covered in dressings, as that's where ALL of the skin they used to graft the rest of my burned body came from.

When I first arrived at St John's I was immobile. I basically stayed in bed unless I needed the toilet, in which case I was carefully placed into a hoist and winched onto a commode, the same kind of hoist used to get old age pensioners in and out of baths. I dreaded having to use the commode. Even though I knew the fantastic nurses on the ward had seen it all before, I would say that those were the lowest moments, having to use that thing.

My four stubby fingers on my right hand were still agonisingly painful to move and the thumb on the same hand was still heavily dressed, and I couldn't bend it. The scarring to the left of my chin now resembled a big pink patch of bubble wrap.

However, visitors poured in when I moved to St John's. As well as my mum, my sister, my dad, my uncle Ron, my gran and my big mad uncle Gaby, I was visited by my friends Maggie and John, Tony, Davie, Jenny, Big Alex Mcechnie, Andy Codona, Davie's mum and dad, long time family friends Eleanor and Drew and my cousin William. It was in St John's that I first met my dad's new wife, Susan, which I wasn't ready for at the time but it has worked out OK anyway. I also received a visit from Banksie's dad, one of the Hibees who I attended games with as a teenager, and of course my old friends and flatmates Martin and Eric came in to visit me too, as well as my mate Big Al. I'm not sure what everyone thought of the state of me when they came to see me in St John's, as everybody was so encouraging and positive to me, but they must have been shocked to see the once tall and handsome Ian wrapped up in bandages with his legs mostly missing. If it did bother them then to their credit they didn't let it show.

Some nights I had so many visitors that they had to wait their turn and see me in shifts. I was in big demand! I sincerely apologise if I have neglected to mention anyone else who came to visit me there then I apologise, all my visits were greatly appreciated.

Chapter 26
Humpty Put Back Together Again

My surgery at St John's commenced when the brilliant plastic surgeon Mr Butterworth, who was my consultant, and his crack team got to work on removing the thick black crust from my chest and stomach and putting skin grafts, again taken from my back, over it. This operation went well and I even got someone to bring me in a McDonald's that evening after I woke up, as the anaesthetic had given me the munchies. It tasted great, but I vomited it up almost straight away and was pretty sick for the rest of the night and part of the next day. In fact I felt awful and was dreading the next operation because of this.

A nurse called Anne from the ward had to sit with me all night after that operation and periodically had to use cotton wool on my newly grafted chest to soak up blood clots and things that might stop it assimilating with my body properly. To this point that was the most painful thing I had experienced. It was excruciating. But it had to be done and I don't envy the poor nurse who had to perform this task on me.

To make matters worse, as they had needed to 'harvest' my back again for skin to graft on my chest, I now had a huge dressing on my back to help it heal more quickly, and it was stitched on to me.

By now I had been given my first own wheelchair by the mobility centre, a little red electric number which I propelled and steered with my good left hand using a little joystick. Though I was still confined to my room for my own good other than when the nurses took me for a shower bath, it was good to know that it was there. Within a few weeks I was able to slowly struggle out of my bed and into my wheelchair to go across to my sink and shave. Shaving was painful and difficult thanks to the 'bubble wrap' scarring under my chin on the left and took some time, but I also learned to brush my teeth again using an electric toothbrush with an extra thick handle. It may sound simple, but teaching myself to do those things again felt great and made me eager to do more.

Every day the kind nurses changed all my dressings and spoke to me. Everyone who looked after me in St John's, from the lovely tea ladies right up to the consultant surgeon, was immense. My chest and abdomen seemed to be taking the skin graft OK, and the black crust had now been replaced with thick purple scarring that I was told would fade with time. Unfortunately, even when grafted you lose most, if not all, of the feeling as the original nerve endings are gone, meaning I could literally brush my fingers over my chest and stomach and not feel a thing. I was as lucky with my chest burns in that my nipples weren't burned, as I've always found them to be one of my more erogenous zones.

Taking the dressing off my back where I had been grafted was a different matter altogether. I'll always remember I was listening to the album 'Heathen Chemistry' by Oasis when four nurses came in to take it off. As it was stitched on it had to be literally torn off my back, so I lay face down while the nurses removed it. It was fucking agony! Far worse than the procedure used on my chest after it's operation. I cried again, but gritted my teeth as the nurses pulled off the dressing. Imagine someone tearing fish hooks out of your back and you're on the way to imagining how sore this was. I cried in agony and wept as Oasis belted out 'Songbird', but by the time the next track came on the dressing was off.

I felt so relieved. My nurses looked just as upset as me, one of them was even crying at having to inflict so much pain on a man who had already suffered so much, but the procedure was entirely necessary and had to be done. I still needed a minor operation to remove staples from my chest site as well as major surgery to save my knee, but after that incident they spared me further agony and knocked me out with anaesthetic to remove the staples from my chest and cleaned my wounds.

I had been a lucky man in Dublin, only one in ten victims with 65 per cent burns survives such injuries, but I was going to need considerable further help from Lady Luck if my recovery and rehabilitation was to continue. The plan was that after the operation to my knee I would be transferred to the Astley Ainslie Hospital in Edinburgh where I would then be given occupational therapy, physiotherapy and be fitted for prosthetic limbs.

In the interim I actually found my stay at St John's rather pleasant after a while. The food was good, essential to a happy stay in hospital, my visitors kept my spirits up and between my friends and family I had acquired quite an impressive multimedia entertainment system. Well, for a guy in hospital it was a godsend. I had the hospital TV, two video recorders, a DVD player, CD player, a PlayStation and a PS2. I couldn't really play the games consoles that well because of my still painful swollen fingers, but I did have a few laughs playing against Martin and then my sister at the shooting game, Medal of Honour. The highlight came when I got a perfect copy of 'Lord of the Rings - the Two Towers', on DVD and watched it in the dark on my own late one night. For those two and a bit hours I forgot all about being severely disabled, and even when the film finished and I remembered my situation, I didn't feel so bad and slept like a top. One more operation to go, then it was on to the rehabilitation hospital, new legs, and a new life.

Chapter 27
The Need To Know

When my dear friends bought me a mobile phone to replace the one stolen by the scumbags in Dundalk I was well chuffed. As well as being able to bombard my friends with silly or insulting joke texts, I decided that I wanted to speak to Girl X again. She had kept tabs on my progress through my dad and his wife and, as I could hardly remember anything about the fire other than knowing it hadn't been an accident, I texted her and she called me back, in tears. We stayed in touch throughout my time in St John's and she made it clear that she wanted to come over and look after me on a permanent basis. We talked a lot on the phone and I remembered how happy we had been for that fateful ten days before the fire. She offered to come over and live with me when I got out, which felt great to hear but when I asked her about the fire all she said was, 'Try not to think about it.'

I received a visit from Livingston police one weekend in St John's, a friendly cop named PC Corner, who knew my sister from school. He read me the Gardaí's account of that dreadful night that they had managed to cobble together from all those present. Not easy considering the state everyone had been in. That jogged my memory a bit, but not enough, and I couldn't really tell him much more than he already knew. Then he mentioned three men's names as he read another statement. I recognised the names of my two housemates as they had, of course, initially been at the party, but the third name chilled me though I couldn't place the guy at the time. I asked the policeman if he could come back in a few months as I had a lot of surgery and rehab still to do, and to be honest hearing that third guy's name had scared me. The policeman was brilliant about it and left.

I sustained no mental damage after the fire and subsequent period in hospital, but I did kind of lose my wits a little for a while afterwards. I wasn't as sharp as I used to be. I think the trauma caused that. I repeated the suspicious name the policeman had given me to Girl X and she hesitated then simply answered, 'A fella we were drinking with that night.' I now remembered this man's aggressive behaviour on the Christmas Eve but for the moment that was all I could remember, though I was sure now that he was involved in my attempted murder. If he was then I was sure that by now my housemates would have busted him, but I didn't want to think about that now. I still had my life to rebuild.

Chapter 28
Make Or Break

My last operation to try and save my knee loomed. The head of orthopaedics, Mr Quaba, came to see me the night before. He very honestly told me that if this operation wasn't successful then I would probably spend the rest of my life in a wheelchair. I was thankful for his honesty. He also told me that if it was successful I should have no problems walking in future. I had already been given the basics of what they were going to do to patch over the huge bit of exposed bone below my remaining knee. It sounded ambitious to say the least. They intended to take a piece of flesh about the area of a twenty pound note from my left forearm and graft it over the exposed bone on my leg. There was more. So that the flesh could get a blood supply, they were going to take an artery, also from my left forearm, and use that to 'plumb in' the new flesh on my leg via the back of my knee. It had been done successfully before. This time there was nothing my family, my friends or I could do to influence the outcome. It was make or break time for my knee and my future hopes of one day walking again. It was in the hands of the surgeons now, and God.

I was scared the night before this operation, but a pre operation med helped me sleep the night before. I remember the now familiar procedure of anaesthetic, when the anaesthetist tells you to count to ten but I never made it up to five. Mr Butterworth and his team operated on me for over eleven hours. I actually recall waking up when they were bandaging me up afterwards, I was still off my head on the anaesthetic though, and I had been given an epidural to reduce suffering afterwards. I actually swore at the surgeons, telling them, 'Don't put any fucking tape on my skin this time,' which thankfully they did not. I spent the next two days after the operation on the high dependency ward as a precaution, but all I really remember about that is vomiting blackcurrant juice all over the nurse after he had advised me not to drink as I might be sick.

I was sick for a few days after this operation, but ultimately it was a great success. Even today the 'flap' they put on my leg looks cool, as does the loch ness monster style scar on my arm where they took the artery. I was confined to my bed again for a while after this sixteenth major operation (prior to the fire I had never had an operation in my life) which was a little frustrating, as by now I was able to get in and out of my wheelchair at will, wash, shave, clean my teeth and even go over and change DVDs and CDs. I still had MRSA though, so was barrier nursed the whole time. With the exception of when I went for a shower-bath, I didn't leave that room in St John's for two-and-a-half months. My leg operation was a complete success and I celebrated my 25th birthday in St John's, with visits from all the usual suspects, even enjoying two cans of chilled lager.

I was encouraged to eat lots after my operations, as my skin grafts might literally have fallen off without substantial nutrition. This wasn't easy in the day or so after the operations but it helped that St John's food was so good. Davie and my other mates brought me in a kebab on a Friday and I started to put on weight. Naturally I started looking fat too, as I was either sitting down or lying down 24 hours, 7 days a week.

When I first went to St John's I had been unable to wear clothes other than bright orange shorts provided by the hospital, but as my wounds healed slowly I was able to start wearing the odd loose t-shirt instead of bandages.

One sad irony though was my dressing changes. As my burns started to heal, the dressing changing procedure got more and more excruciatingly painful. In the end they started giving me entonox, or 'gas and air', the stuff they give to women in labour, to help with the pain and it certainly did, in fact I often ended up in fits of giggles as the nurses painstakingly changed the dressings on my hands, arms, back, front and what was left of my legs. The only time the entonox didn't work was when they took the stitches out of my knee when I was having a shower bath. I screamed in agony, it was so sore, I can still remember the feeling today. On that occasion I kind of collapsed from the optimistic determined guy everyone said I was, into a crying, shaking wreck, naked in the bath, scarred and purple all over with no legs. And oh, that's how I felt, too. Everything was getting on top of me at that moment but the kind nurses, realising the state I was in, gave me a diazepam and told me to leave it under my tongue. I soon calmed down. That was the last time I was ever to break down in such a manner. I think being cooped up in that room for over two months had just got to me, but I woke up refreshed and felt good again.

Chapter 29
An Inspired Visit

I was asked by the hospital social worker if I wanted a visit from an amputee so that I could ask them questions. Initially I baulked at the idea, but my pals and family had heard of the amputee woman in question and urged me to give it a go. So Olivia visited me one evening.

The first thing I noticed was that a beautiful blonde woman was standing in my room doorway. It was only after that that I noticed she was in fact a quadruple amputee. I had big hang ups about the way I now looked, but the fact that I first noticed her as a beautiful woman rather than as an amputee made me realise that maybe things weren't going to be so bad after all. Olivia answered all my questions and filled me with hope for the future. She even knew some people at my beloved Hibs and asked who my favourite player was. I was to find out why she asked that later. Her coming to see me was instrumental in my recovery and I am eternally grateful to her. We are still good friends today.

I did get some physiotherapy at St John's, though obviously I was a bit limited in my movements. The most valuable physiotherapy was when the physio would come in and stretch my right hand. It had become almost claw like and needed to be stretched back out flat. This was more uncomfortable than painful, and after a few weeks of this my right hand slowly got better, although the tips of my 'new' fingers still felt strange and tingly.

The physios also measured me for pressure garments. These are skin tight Lycra garments worn directly over the skin that over time reduce the effects of scarring and flatten bad scars. I had shorts, a shirt, gloves and a horrible chinstrap. I didn't see the use of these at the time but now I see the effect they have had in fading my scars, particularly the horrible 'bubble wrap' under my chin.

The care I received from everyone at St John's was first class from beginning to end. Now, as patched up as I could be but still with a couple of small niggling wounds, I was transferred to Sutherland Ward of the Astley Ainslie Hospital at the end of April 2003.

All my stuff was packed up in big plastic bags and I went down to the ambulance. That was my first time outside in two months. The ambulance journey was uneventful and it was pissing down with rain when we reached the hospital. On the amputee ward, I was thankfully given my own single room again because of the MRSA I was still carrying all over my body. Because of this my visitors had to wear pink aprons. Astley Ainslie is an old, old building but the grounds are beautiful, especially in spring and summer. I was allowed outside here and could sit out in the huge garden and watch rabbits running around during the day and foxes at night. I was raring to get going, get rehabilitated and get my new legs.

Chapter 30
Astley Ainslie

At first things went slowly at Astley. Like the other hospitals I had been in, the staff were just amazing, every last one of them. I still had to use a commode in my room as I couldn't use the main toilets because of my super bug infection and I initially wasn't allowed into physio because of it either, but the kind physios came and gave me some exercises to be getting on with in my room.

My mum, my dad, and Tony were the most frequent visitors when I was in here, as Tony works in Edinburgh. I got a cheap calls package from O2 which meant I was able to phone Girl X. We talked lots, and it was clear we still fancied each other. The idea of getting out of hospital and getting a house with that girl who had made me so happy just sounded like heaven. She planned to come and visit me in June. I was pleased and that perked me up, I really wanted to see her.

Hibs had been utter crap since I had returned to Scotland. They had ended up in the bottom six of the SPL again and had been knocked out of the Scottish Cup after a replay by Dunfermline. Total humiliation. To make matters worse, Celtic lost the league to Rangers by one goal, Rangers being managed by our ex manager Alex McLeish. Rangers won the cup too, and then Celtic narrowly lost the UEFA Cup Final to FC Porto 3-2. I saw all these games from hospital. I'm no Celtic fan but having watched every round of the UEFA cup I really wanted them to win it, not just to shove it up Rangers, but because most of my friends support Celtic.

Eventually I was allowed to go over to physio and do the exercises that would hopefully get me walking again. Initially they put me on a tilt table, which is an early way of getting people who haven't been upright for ages, upright. It felt strange at first but it also felt amazing. There were two physios on at a time, plus a physiotherapy assistant. The full timer was called Lyndsay and the other post was shared between Rona and Catriona.

They gave me every encouragement and were very positive but, though

Burnt

I was keen to walk, I didn't see the point in doing some of the exercises at first. They seemed irrelevant, but I pushed on. The next step in walking rehabilitation (every pun intended) is using a PAM aid. These are essentially inflatable prosthesis within a metal cage that you can do a limited amount of walking on and that also get your 'stumps' used to having pressure on them again. My sister Angela saw me walking with these things on a big walking frame and almost cried. It was a small step, but a step in the right direction.

It was great being able to go outside into the grounds and stuff at Astley Ainslie, particularly as it was summer time. One Saturday I had a visit from Davie, Tony and Martin, whom I hadn't seen since St John's. I had recently demanded a manual wheelchair and been given one to replace my electric one as I thought I needed the exercise. I was getting fatter. We went for a walk in the grounds and Martin pushed me for a while. He accidentally let go of my wheelchair as we were going down a hill and I went absolutely hurtling down it towards the grass. I don't think he had handled a wheelchair before and looking back it was hilarious, no harm done.

Chapter 31
Worthwhile Distractions

One Tuesday in May I received a surprise visitor. My Hibs hero, Mixu Paatelainen, turned up at my room, obviously arranged by Olivia. I was overjoyed to meet one of my heroes in the flesh. He had to wear a pink apron.

What a morale booster! He stayed and spoke to me for about an hour and gave me a shirt signed by the entire squad! I asked him about who the hardest opponents were and things like that and he didn't have a bad thing to say about anyone. He told me the highlight of his career was his hat-trick against Hearts when we humiliated them 6-2 in October 2000, and he even expressed regret at us losing the 2001 Cup Final to Celtic, saying it was one of the hardest games he has ever played in. He gave me a hug and left. Mixu had actually just left Hibs and went on to manage Cowdenbeath. I truly wish him every possible success in the future. He's an absolute gent and his visit lifted my spirits no end. He's a damn good Hibby, too.

I got another morale booster when my sister gave me her PC to put in my room. I had no Internet but I had Championship Manager and that filled up the weekends. There's only so many times you can win the treble and Champion's League with Hibs though and I soon got bored, and was delighted when the hospital let me have an Internet connection.

I had an account with a well-known 'internet for idiots' company who offered flat rate Internet access. I mainly used the computer for downloading music illegally and for using my ISP's handy football chat room. This was great fun, winding people up all day, and I even made a couple of cool 'pals' through it. However, I was continually being warned as the company had very strict conditions of service. Myself and another guy from Edinburgh called Geoff were causing absolute mayhem on this ISP. We were cloning people's accounts, winding people up and generally being a nuisance. It got so bad that three or four other users started to do what we were doing and soon you didn't know WHOM you were talking too. Eventually after three warnings the company terminated my account but I got let back on, only after sending them a signed fax pledging never to muck about on the site again. My PC was a great help to me in hospital. It gave me a window to the world and some much needed respite from physio, which seemed to be going nowhere.

Chapter 32
Limbo

The worst stage of being an amputee is not amputation itself, nor recovering from surgery. It's the 'limbo' period when you are waiting on your wounds to heal properly before you can begin the process of measuring, casting, fitting, and then walking with parallel bars, zimmer frames, crutches and ultimately walking sticks. That's the soul-destroying part. The waiting. You feel as if you're life is on hold and there's nothing you or the doctors and physios can do about it. My attitude took a slump in this period despite all the encouragement and support I received from friends, family and staff. I started getting bizarre flashbacks.

An amputee charity, the Murray Foundation, arranged for me to see a counsellor. The Murray Foundation was set up by Rangers chairman David Murray to provide support and advice for Scottish amputees, and they provide an invaluable service. I was able to talk through all the stress I had about life, what had happened and some more personal stuff with the counsellor, indeed they even provided some of my family with counselling too as my losing my legs was like a bereavement to my family and close friends.

This counselling had two positive outcomes. Firstly, it helped me focus my mind on what I should do to rebuild my shattered life. Secondly, getting stuff off my chest freed up my mind to think more about what happened to me in Ireland. It helped me remember being beaten up and whacked over the head.

All this time I stayed in touch with the girl from Ireland. She came over to visit me that June and really lifted my spirits. It was like we had carried on from where we had left off the previous Christmas Eve. We planned to get a place together here when I got out of hospital. This gave me something to aim for in terms of getting my legs and getting out of hospital. I couldn't wait now.

After she went home to Ireland I got a surprise one Sunday morning: a phone call from my old Dundalk housemates. It was great to hear from them. Girl X had given them my number and they had obviously been up drinking all night, but we had a good laugh on the phone. I had been kind of disappointed not to hear from them up until now but they explained that they just hadn't known what to say, understandable since they hadn't known me that long before the fire. My housemate's sister texted me too just to see how I was doing and I was also still in touch with my old boss Neil.

Chapter 33
Staying Sane

Bath time at Astley Ainslie was by now a bit of a running joke. The kind staff still let me have gas and air for dressing changes and baths, even though I didn't need it, so bath time involved being hoisted into the bath by a nurse and bathing listening to Beat 106 whilst having the occasional blast of gas and air. Most therapeutic. Eventually I told them I didn't need the stuff anymore as it was making me tired.

Music helped me a lot during my time in Astley Ainslie, both the stuff I downloaded and the few CDs I still had (I never got round to getting my CD collection back from Dundalk, nor any of my other possessions). I even started to like Pink Floyd, a band that I had hitherto hated with a passion. I didn't listen to much dance music as it reminded me too much of the fact that I wouldn't be able to dance the way that I used to ever again. That feeling wouldn't last forever though.

All this time I was still piling on weight because of my inactive lifestyle and from the takeaway food I was often eating, as I didn't like the hospital food there, though give the cooks their due. When I complained they offered me the use of the staff canteen instead and I gladly accepted. The weight still piled on with no sign yet of me being able to walk it off, and what exercise I could do with dumbbells and in physio did little to stop me ballooning. The manual wheelchair did however start making me a little stronger and fitter, and I was soon a dab hand at controlling it, even managing wheelies and sixpence turns.

I was still wearing pressure garments to bring my scars down, including the silly but highly effective chinstrap. They were pretty uncomfortable to wear in the middle of summer though.

I received a phone call from the Gardaí while I was in that hospital, but I had visitors around when they called so I asked them to call back. They didn't phone me back.

I was starting to see why I had been given some of the exercises that I had earlier deemed to be pointless and silly. I finally figured out what they were all about when I was asked to sit on a balance cushion that wobbled, while the physiotherapist threw a ball for me to catch. The cushion wobbled, putting me off balance when I moved to catch the ball, but that was the whole point. Building up the muscles that I hadn't used since Christmas Eve, six months previously. Slowly but surely I got better at it and was able to do more exercises.

Eventually I was deemed to be sufficiently healed and ready to be cast for new limbs, although my scars were still pretty horrific. I don't remember much about the casting process at that time, though I remember Lyndsay the physio asking me if I would like a custom design built into my below knee leg socket, and I thought this was a great idea and asked to have a Hibs top laminated into it. My prosthetist, Francine, made a superb job of laminating it into the socket and when I got the leg it looked well smart. When I first saw my new legs I was so excited, though they did look a little odd.

Most people ask for cosmetic foam around the prosthesis to make it look like a real leg but I asked just to have the titanium poles going directly into my shoes, like my friend Olivia had as, the way I saw it, I had no reason to hide my disability. Not having cosmetic foam on my legs would also mean they could be repaired a lot more easily should anything go wrong with them. I had my legs, everything was going according to plan. Then disaster struck again.

One Saturday morning in August 2003 I started to feel very sick indeed. I was sweating, had the shivers, a splitting headache and I was in pain because of bright light. My mum, and my auntie Kath, who was over from Germany, got a taxi from Livingston to see if I was OK. I got sicker and sicker as the day wore on and as my temperature rocketed it became clear that the rehabilitation ward I was on wasn't where I should be.

I was transferred to accident and emergency, combined assessment at Edinburgh Royal Infirmary to find out the source of this dangerous mystery infection. I honestly thought my number was up this time, I thought I was going to have a heart attack, but the staff at ERI were brilliant and I was lucky that the duty consultant orthopaedic surgeon there that day had been part of the team that looked after me in St John's.

It was decided that I should be moved back to the burns unit in St John's so that my consultants could have a look at what was wrong. The duty guy had obviously seen something in my X-ray that concerned him. I was lucky that he was there. By evening I actually felt a little better but I would have to wait until Monday to find out for certain what was wrong. It felt like getting to the second last square on snakes and ladders only to find that it's a big long snake that takes you right back down. It was a major setback. The staff in the burns unit were pleased to see me but I don't think I was as good a patient as I had been the first time, as by now I had been at Astley Ainslie for over three months and was used to going outside for fresh air, talking to other patients and mucking around on my PC. Being back in that one room was frustrating. I just wanted them to sort me out so I could get back to rehab.

On the Monday my brilliant consultant informed me that the reason I had been ill was because of a bone disease in my right leg, called osteomyelitis. It was basically a bone disease that makes your bone die and turn into a kind of ivory. You may remember that when I stayed in Dundalk I had started to get very sore legs a lot of the time. My family were asked if I had had sore legs before, as they had seen small signs of this disease when they amputated my legs, but of course no one was aware of this as I hadn't complained to anyone. I had just put my sore legs down to too much walking or football. I had probably been developing this disease for a considerable time and I was told it was probably from years of jumping on and off electric picking trucks and forklifts in my warehouse days, particularly as I had mostly worked in chilled warehouses.

The good news was that they only needed to shave a tiny fraction off the end of my leg, meaning that my knee would still be OK. A minor operation. I was still scared though, not of the operation as by now these were becoming almost second nature, but of being sick from the anaesthetic again. Thankfully they knew of my concerns and gave me slightly different anaesthetic this time and, after this operation, low and behold, I woke up and felt great, tucking into a full dinner and then phoning Girl X and all my family and friends to tell them how brilliant I felt. Another setback had tried to ruin my recovery, but again it had been overcome. I did have some trouble getting straight back to Astley Ainslie because of red tape, but my family sorted that out.

I also soon hoped to get my legs. Girl X came over to see me again in August and it was great to see her. We had a lovely time away at a hotel for the night then on the next night we went and stayed at my dad's house. This was my first weekend away from hospital in eight months and the Friday night was brilliant, though it tired me out so much that I was in bed very early at my dad's house the next evening. It was brilliant of my dad and his wife to let us stay, though his was the only house out of everyone I knew who we could go to with me in the wheelchair as it was a bungalow. Considering I hadn't ever been in his house before, the weekend went well, though I was understandably very nervous.

Chapter 34
Happy Ever After?

Girl X moved over to Scotland permanently on 11 September. We had got engaged when she was over in August and I was really looking forward to getting out and setting up house with her.

Life seemed so simple. We were in love and even planned to get married in October 2004. My family and friends were pleased for us, though for some reason she snapped my SIM card when I received a text from someone in Dundalk. From then on it was clear that she didn't want me talking to anyone in Dundalk except her family, which I didn't mind as they were always very positive and encouraging to me on the phone.

At weekends when I got out of hospital we stayed with my dad and his wife as I was still technically homeless, but the social work department at the hospital were by now busy trying to arrange for a house for me. My family and friends obviously wanted me to move back to Livingston, but I still wanted a fresh start and chose Edinburgh, as that would save me lots of long trips to the prosthetics centre, which was also in Edinburgh. Edinburgh was also where my beloved team played.

Girl X came in to see me every day during the week and we stayed at my dad's at weekends. I spent most of my time there panting and puffing on the sofa as it was an exceptionally hot summer, and with my skin grafts I could only really sweat from my head and back. The heat was terribly uncomfortable and I had an electric fan pointed at me almost all of the time when I wasn't on the move.

I don't know how she did it, but Girl X managed to speed up the housing process and I was offered a two bedroom flat in a nice area of South Edinburgh, not too far from the hospital. I viewed it with Derek, the marvellous hospital social worker, and accepted it there and then. I had a few thousand pounds in the bank now thanks to kind donations from my old boss Neil, the Irish dole office who had backdated my money to 24 December 2002 until I left Ireland on 18 February, the good people of my old housing estate of

Burnt

Craigshill in Livingston, in particular the Stirrup Stane pub who gave me a thousand pounds, and money collected by my friends from their work. My pals Maggie and John even walked the West Highland Way and got sponsored to do it, giving the money to me. With this money I was able to get everything we needed for the house, and just as well as the DSS gave me barely seven hundred pounds with which to do it. I was also able to buy some much-needed new clothes, and have a few good days out with my girlfriend. Now that we had a house, all that was needed was for me to get used to my legs and then to get on with my life. Alas that was not to be...

The wound at the bottom of my right leg where I had had the recent further amputation broke down in physio in late September. It wasn't anyone's fault, the reason was that an extra shard of bone had been growing off my tibia and pushing outwards, stretching the skin. I was going to need yet another operation. I expected to be taken straight back to St John's, but as I now had a house it was agreed that I should go home first for a while to have a much-needed rest. I was told to go home and wait for a letter giving me a date to go into St John's for one last plastics operation. Though I was still in a wheelchair and had to be visited by the district nurse every second day to have the leg wound dressed, I was finally out of hospital in October. I had been in for ten months and had had seventeen major operations all in all. Lucky to be alive was the understatement of the century.

Chapter 35
Home To Rest

It was so good to finally be out of hospital. I had barely walked ten yards with my new legs before this setback happened, but I expected to go back into St John's after Christmas for that last operation and then to complete my rehabilitation and get walking by my birthday in April. In the meantime I had my beautiful girlfriend to look after me and friends and family to catch up with socially, rather than in a hospital environment.

I had been unable to attend Hibs' first big game of the season against Hearts as I hadn't been well enough to go, but I had seen the game on television. Hibs had won 1-0 with a last gasp Garry O'Connor strike, despite playing most of the match with ten men after Grant Brebner's red card. My first visit to Easter Road since that Aberdeen game was against Celtic. We lost 1-2 despite taking the lead through Matt Doumbe, but it was such a good feeling to be back watching Hibs again. I had to sit in the main stand as my old stand, the East, wasn't wheelchair accessible. Strangely at this game I didn't even notice that there were any away fans until Celtic took the lead, but even then the loudest singing was from our fans, ridiculing the Celtic fans by singing 'You only sing when you're winning'.

I was disappointed at the poor atmosphere in this stand and was even asked to 'Shhh' a couple of times when I instinctively tried to start a song. Still, the view was a bit better in the main stand and it was handy for gesticulating and shouting abuse at opposing players. I distinctly remember Alan Thomson pulling a 'spazzy' face at the wheelchair section after he had scored Celtic's usual dodgy penalty. So Hibs had lost, but considering I never thought that I was going to see them again it was still great to be back. Already I was dreaming of getting my legs and getting back on to the East Stand where I belonged.

We went to several more games, though the next memorable one was the League Cup quarter final in December, again against Celtic. Celtic took the lead but we came out on top 2-1 with goals from a Grant Brebner spot kick and a late Kevin Thomson strike. It was freezing but I didn't care. We were in the cup semi-finals now. How great it would be if we won the cup after everything that had happened to me, I thought.

On 17 September 2003 my mates Davie and Jenny had their second child, a wee girl called Kerry. I am now Kerry's godfather, which makes me proud.

Up until Christmas week 2003 my girlfriend and I had a great time together, she really looked after me. Martin came round one night for a drink and we all got pissed and listened to blaring rock music, so loud that my upstairs neighbour came down to complain.

Christmas week came around again and what a difference a year makes. We planned to have dinner with all my friends on Christmas Day in Livingston at Davie's house. We met my mum, my sister and my gran in Morningside in a pub the day before Christmas Eve. I was very ill and hadn't been able to eat a thing in days, but I still made it out. We had a lovely meal, and before my girlfriend and I left my gran shouted me over and gave me a big kiss. That made me smile. She had been to visit me in hospital in Livingston but it was good to see her again. We were all looking forward to having a nice quiet uneventful Christmas after the living hell that had been last year, but it wasn't to be. Next morning my mum phoned me with the terrible sad news that my gran had died at home. Christmas seemed to be cursed again. It must have been awful for my mother, particularly at that time of year being the anniversary of my accident.

I was starting to hate Christmas with a passion. And it got worse.

I had to be rushed to hospital on Christmas morning 2003! This time it was nothing as serious as the year before, but I was still very sick. I couldn't hold anything down, let alone water, and I was in utter agony with stomach pains. Christmas morning in accident and emergency is no fun I assure you, and that added a great deal of stress and worry for me and my family, on top of the devastating news we had had about my gran the day before, plus the fact it was a year ago that I had been rushed into hospital. The hospital staff managed to sort me out and it was found to be a painkiller I was on called Diclofenac which had caused my second painful Christmas in a row.

To me it was like one big sick joke. Fuck Christmas, I thought. I was too ill to go to Davie's for dinner, and in any case I was still unable to eat so that was two Christmases on the trot that I got no dinner. Though I was also thankful that I wasn't to be roasted again that year.

My gran's funeral was on Hogmanay and was very well attended. It gave a sombre mood to the Hogmanay party that I attended with Girl X and my friends, but we nevertheless had a great time, and it was great to party with all my friends again. Annoyingly I couldn't get upstairs to use the toilet and had to pee in a jug downstairs. This of course didn't bother my amazing friends, but it bothered me. Standing up to pee is part of being a man!

Chapter 36
Quest For Justice

I had spent the last couple of months of 2003 and the first few months of 2004 badgering the Irish Government to do something about the scumbags who had done this to me. At first my torrent of emails and letters appeared to have been ignored. By now I remembered the attack, but was still unsure of a few details. Unfortunately I hadn't remembered some of the details I have mentioned earlier. That shouldn't have mattered though.

In January 2004, my mum and Girl X went over to Dundalk to see the Gardaí in person. The Gardaí were very shocked to see my mum. They tried to fob her off but they eventually agreed to see her. Two Gards, and I know their names, told my mum that I had been the victim of a hideous violent crime, that they knew who at least one of the attackers was and that he would be arrested within the week. They also told my mum that there was a certain natural justice in that part of the world so that the scumbag(s) could probably expect retribution as well as a prison sentence. The only witness to this was Girl X and I doubt she would back this up now.

My mum was treated well by my girlfriend's family, particularly her older brother who picked them up from the airport. My mum had taken photographs of me in my burned legless state wearing only boxer shorts to shock the Gards into doing something about it and they said they would. And we thought they would. The Gards themselves admitted the investigation had been cocked up since day one.

It seemed as if the Gardaí were finally going to do something about it all. The brave Garda who saved me from the fire and apprehended a suspect at the scene was mysteriously moved, my girlfriend told me. The case was taken up by a superintendent and I was hopeful of a swift resolution to the case, a jail sentence for my attackers and the criminal injuries compensation that I now desperately needed as there was no way I could go back to my old line of work.

Burnt

The Gards asked me if I knew a man by the name of SM (full name withheld for legal reasons) for some reason, the neighbour I mentioned earlier who had eyeballed me outside my girlfriend's house, and they also asked for my Irish mobile phone number, and my girlfriend's Irish number, neither of which I could remember, but my girlfriend could so she gave the superintendent the numbers over the phone.

Chapter 37
More Waiting

January 2004 passed and I still hadn't had a letter from St John's about my operation. I was getting depressed. From earning £340 a week in my last Scottish job I was now supporting my girlfriend and I on much less than I was used to as I was now on benefits. The fact we had to get taxis everywhere certainly didn't help either. I just wanted to get my operation over so that I could start walking again. It started to get me down.

My sprits were lifted when Girl X, Tony and I went through to Hampden Park in Glasgow to see Hibs take on Rangers in the League Cup semi-final. We were underdogs by a long way. They had already knocked us out of the Scottish Cup rather easily a few weeks before. We were basically a team of under-21s and missing our two best players, and Rangers were the League Champions and holders of the cup and multi millionaires, having just signed Dutch skipper Frank De Boer on loan.

Only about seven thousand of my fellow Hibs fans made it through to Glasgow for this midweek game, so we were outnumbered three to one by their fans. We still out sang them all night. Rangers took the lead but we equalised through Stephen Dobbie and eventually beat them on penalties, their new 'star' signing De Boer missing the decisive penalty. The Rangers fans choked the exits while our fans sang and danced as the tannoy blasted out '500 Miles' by the Proclaimers, a tune synonymous with Hibs. We were in the final now and would face crappy Livingston. Surely a cup win was on the cards. The funniest part of that night was extra policemen being drafted in to cover the Hibs DISABLED section, as me, Tony and a few other lads were screaming so much abuse at Rangers diddy men Maurice Ross and Michael Ball.

The final against Livingston on 14 March 2004 is a day I'll never forget, for all the wrong reasons. Davie's dad drove us all in Tony's van. We had four tickets. My girlfriend and I had tickets for the Hibs disabled section while my pals Maggie and Tony, both Celtic fans, ended up with tickets for the Livi end. They only came to have a laugh with us anyway and we all wanted Hibs to win of course.

The day started badly, Davie's dad reversing Tony's van into a concrete bollard at Carfinn Hibs club, where we had stopped to get drunk for the game. There were hundreds of Hibs fans in the club and we had a great time in there before the game, singing and chanting but, as usual with Hibs, that's as good as the Hampden day out got. Tony and Maggie walked into the Livingston end steaming drunk and started to roar Hibs songs, and they were soon chucked out.

My girlfriend and I arrived just after kick off and the stadium was a sight to see. We had about forty thousand fans to Livingston's six or seven thousand. Predictably, Hibs, who were overwhelming favourites, lost the final 2-0. Humiliation. It got worse.

On leaving the stadium, my wheelchair's front wheels caught on some TV cables, catapulting me forwards out and onto the concrete floor. I took my full weight through my right leg. It was torture, absolute agony. Event security staff and the St John's Ambulance men were on the scene straight away and advised me to go to A&E, but the last thing I wanted to do was go back to hospital, particularly after watching such a lame display by my team. I chose instead just to go home and go to bed, but I had such pain in my leg that I had to go to hospital anyway two days later for an x-ray and to be given really good painkillers. I thought this might speed up the process of getting into St John's, but it did nothing of the sort. In fact, it would mean I had to wait even longer for my new legs.

On Valentine's Day my girlfriend and I had stayed in a posh Edinburgh hotel for the night, having a great time. I got a call that morning though. My granddad had died. He had been ill for a while and had been a resident of a war veteran's home in Edinburgh. I think my gran dying only a few weeks before knocked the stuffing out of him. He was a veteran of WWII, having spent four years in a prisoner of war camp after being captured when the Nazis invaded the island of Crete in 1941. His unit was part of the garrison.

This was a new low for me. I had hardly seen my grandparents in the preceding couple of years and we were all grief stricken. When told of what had happened to me in Dundalk, my grandfather hadn't spoken a word to anyone for two whole weeks. Again this must have been particularly bad for my mum. When I put the phone down after the call I cried in the hotel room.

After I composed myself I had a strange premonition. Hibs weren't going to lose today. My granddad had been a lifelong Hibs fan and I just kinda knew that we wouldn't lose this game. We went to the match, at which there was much hilarity as Hearts had recently announced a harebrained plan to move into a rugby ground and sell their own stadium to cover their enormous spiralling debts. A rugby ball was even thrown onto the pitch, to the great mirth of the Hibs support.

We sang 'MURRAYFIELD YOU'RE HAVIN' A LAUGH, MURRAYFIELD YOU'RE HAVIN' A LAUGH' to the tune of Tom Hark.

When Derek Riordan put us into the lead with a sublime strike I looked to the heavens and dedicated the goal to my granddad. It mattered little that Hearts equalised and the game was drawn.

Chapter 38
Stress

Livingston police finally came to see me to get a full statement about what had happened. I remembered a lot more now, but still had some blank spots. Stupidly I let my girlfriend influence my statement and looking back that was a mistake. Strangely, she asked me not to mention to the police about her attacking me with the plastic mop that Christmas Eve, which I didn't, as I didn't see it as relevant anyway.

However, the kind Scottish policeman told me that the Gardaí were hopeful of concluding the case imminently and that they were sure they had their man. They had a stack of evidence, and as I mentioned earlier, they knew who had done it, as they had told my mum when she went over to see them. Moreover, Jack Straw, MP, and the late Robin Cook, MP, were involved and had confirmed that the Gardaí had said I had been the victim of an 'appalling crime of violence'. I fully expected these scum to be jailed and to be compensated for my injuries now.

Sadly, Girl X and I split up in July 2004. We hadn't been getting on very well for a while. Her jealousy was getting to me, and I'm sure my own little habits must have been annoying her too. It's never easy breaking up with someone you love and this one was particularly painful as we had been through so much together. But, looking back, we had only known each other for ten days before that fire and it was perhaps a bit ambitious of us to jump straight into living together over here, especially as I was now disabled. I think she must have been awfully homesick too. I decided it was better to be alone than unhappy. I missed her when she went back home, and for about five days I was very down after she left but I was sure I had done the right thing in ending our relationship.

I found consolation by playing online games for a few days to give myself a break from reality, meaning my phone was engaged for ages. My friends and family were sad for me but I've since discovered that some of them weren't entirely convinced that we were suited and they were suspicious about her role in what had happened to me. I didn't understand that.

Five days after she left she phoned my landline. She was obviously out walking somewhere. She told me she was pregnant, which I knew was a lie, but what she said next chilled my blood. She said that she had been 'told' by someone to 'change her story' and was going to make sure I didn't get any justice, or any compensation. I was shocked. Why would she do this? It made no sense. Who 'told' her to change her story?

I hung up after this call and got my number changed straight away, getting a block put on so that I couldn't receive calls from Ireland. My friends Maggie and Jenny were with me with their kids at the time and they stayed an extra few hours to make sure I was OK, which I greatly appreciated. I really didn't get it. What was this all about?

Even more strangely, a week later, the Livingston police came back to see me. They had some more specific questions for me, and also asked me if I was happy with my last statement. Knowing what Robin Cook and Jack Straw had told us, and remembering the wealth of evidence AND what the Gardaí had told my mum, I ratified my statement, though I thought it was a bit strange that the Gardaí had asked for a statement again so soon after she had got home to Dundalk. I should have added the extra things I had remembered, but I didn't think they were important at the time and in any case I was now too upset to think straight. So my statement was virtually unchanged.

It didn't stop there. A couple of weeks later on a Thursday night my mate Robert, who I used to live across the road from, came over. Girl X had his number, and her and some scary sounding guy had been on the phone, demanding Robert deliver me a message. The message was, 'Drop the case about the assault or you will have men in balaclavas at the door and you WILL be shot dead.' They also added that they had managed to 'produce' a 'witness' who claims to have seen me drinking whisky alone whilst smoking a cigarette on the night of the fire. I wasn't worried about that part though, that wouldn't fool even the Gardaí surely. Or would they?

I was scared and decided to phone my dad. Then it got even worse. My ex and her new fiancé had phoned my dad's house too. This time the message was, 'Tell him to drop the case or he'll be killed, it's upsetting Girl X's family.' I haven't a clue what the fuck that was all about, but I of course did no such thing, in fact it made me more determined to see the case settled, but I'm still very puzzled as to why I got threats like this.

We reported the threats to the police here but told them not to bother complaining to the Gardaí as nothing would be done. The police here were great about it, though I had to eventually move house in 2006 because of fear of this and now have a flagged address and police protection. That was the last I ever heard from her. I was sad it had to end that way, but of course, it certainly gets you thinking about things.

My friend Tony has met a few people from Dundalk familiar with my case while he was on holiday abroad. A strange coincidence. These people told him that those responsible for what happened to me are 'scumbags', yet they wouldn't say any more about it. Strange.

Chapter 39
New Beginnings

So I faced up to life on my own, severely disabled. There was still no word on when I was getting my operation and I had now been either sitting or lying down for twenty months. I moped around the house for a couple of weeks doing very little other than seeing my friends and using my PC, though when the new season came I was able to attend a couple of Hibs games with my dad for the first time since 1992 which was cool, though I was starting to get sick of the main stand wheelchair section due to the lack of atmosphere there. I ached to get my legs and get back to the East Stand.

It was also round about now that two things happened that were to have enormous positive impact on my continuing recovery and, indeed, on my future. Firstly, I started going to my local gym. Part of this was vanity as I wanted to get rid of the horrid unattractive man breasts that I had developed, but it was mostly because I knew that it would benefit me greatly to build up my upper body strength, both for propelling and transferring in and out of my wheelchair and for using crutches when I eventually got my new legs.

By this time I was pretty much used to people staring at me in the street in my wheelchair with half my legs missing, so I wasn't at all hung up about going to start training beside a lot of fit, able-bodied people. I got some funny looks at first, but the guy Shug, who gave me my induction, was absolutely brilliant, both in helping me get used to transferring on and off the different equipment, and in encouraging me and talking to me about normal stuff like football. In fact, all the staff at the gym have been very good to me and are lovely people.

The first few times I went to the gym my body ached like hell the next day, and apparently that's what puts most people off after they go a couple of times. I was doing exercises for my chest (two machines), abs, biceps, triceps, back (two machines) and shoulders. I started to go three times a week at first. After a few weeks I started to notice I was getting stronger, but I didn't seem to be losing much weight. However, it lifted the kind of depression I had been under and after a few sessions I started to feel really good rather than getting aches and pains. The music in the gym is usually brilliant too, which is a big help as it makes the session fly by.

After a couple of months of this I noticed a big difference when I transferred from my wheelchair into my bed, the toilet, my shower chair and people's cars. I was even able to get out of my wheelchair into taxis, which meant that the chair could just be lifted in so that I could take less time getting in and out, and make it easier for the driver. My arms were getting strong enough to make this easy.

Going to the gym also got me talking to a lot of people and gave my self-confidence a massive boost. I was fully confident that all this weight lifting would stand me in good stead for when I eventually got my legs. It felt great when family and friends started to comment on how strong I was starting to look. In fact, I wish I had been more into going to the gym when I had been able bodied, not just for the physical benefits, but for the psychological ones too. Going to the gym and all the help and encouragement I received there was to be instrumental in me rebuilding my life.

The second thing that was to change my life happened that September. I had been moping around a bit, getting bored with the same old routine every day, when my mum suggested that I do a college course part time to keep me busy. I initially was dismissive of the idea as I hadn't really been in a classroom since high school, but I phoned a local resource centre and asked what courses were available locally. I was pleasantly surprised to learn that my local university was running a part time course on Scottish military history which was to start the following Monday. I was also eligible to do this course free under the disabled fee waiver scheme. Military history, along with music and football, has always been my specialist topic, in fact it fascinates me. That might have something to do with so many of my family members going back generations having been in one army or another. My mum was a medic with the Royal Army Medical Corps and my dad was in the Royal Engineers.

I was a bag of nerves when I started the course, having been out of the classroom for so long, but I soon found that I had nothing to worry about. The university staff were very helpful and supportive and the course was very, very interesting indeed. The lecturer, Dr Chris Brown, who is a leading expert on William Wallace and Robert Bruce, made the course exciting and informative and we also had a good bunch in the class. I found that all the reading and research I had done over the years was finally coming in useful for something and after a week or two I was soon interrupting and asking questions.

Chris Brown's course was brilliant, and took us up to the union with England in 1707. It was informative and interesting, and it's always a pleasure to be taught by someone who is passionate about what they teach. There was an assessment at the end of the course, one part to be done under exam conditions in the class, the other an essay to be written at home. I was by now confident enough to sit these assessments and when I got my marks back I found that I had got a B. I was jubilant, as were my friends and family. Not bad for what I had been through and for not having been in a classroom for the best part of eleven years.

Starting university part time and going to the gym benefited me greatly, both physically and mentally, in getting my body and brain pushed up a gear, but also socially as I made some good friends and gained some much needed self confidence. These are two of the best decisions I have ever made.

Chapter 40
Mobility

Throughout 2004 I had also been learning to drive using hand controls. This really was essential for my future as I was currently relying on my taxi discount card and lifts from friends to get around. I had a driving assessment while I was in Astley Ainslie and they decided that I was fit to drive, though obviously having no legs and a dodgy right hand any car I drove would need drastic adaptations.

My provisional specified after my assessments that I had to drive an automatic car that wouldn't cut out, with a steering wheel ball so I could steer one handed just like on the forklift trucks I used to drive. This would free my other hand, my dodgy right one, to operate a push/pull accelerate/break system (push in to stop, pull out to accelerate) and also to operate the indicators with my thumb as there was a switch for them on the accelerate/break lever. It sounds complicated but is actually rather easy, far easier than using pedals and it's almost like an arcade game, though obviously you don't get three lives in this case.

My driving instructor was Peter Watt, who specialised in teaching special needs drivers. He is an excellent teacher, patient when he has to be but can also tell you off when you make a bad mistake without hurting your feelings. He is also a very funny man and does stand up comedy. Sometimes my sides ached at the jokes he used to crack while we were out on the road. It initially took me a few lessons to get used to the steering but I soon got the hang of things. I had to do rather a lot of work on my three main manoeuvres, of which I found reversing around a corner the hardest, but by October 2004 I was ready to sit my test.

I was so nervous on the morning of the test that I woke up at 5am, nearly five and a half hours before my test. I had easily passed the theory and hazard perception tests a few weeks previously. They were easy, and the purpose of the theory test is pretty transparent. In a nutshell it raises revenue and helps to keep potentially dangerous drivers off the road. The whole theory test, including the new hazard perception part, which I had never practised, was easy. Pure common sense and basic knowledge. It still felt great to pass it though. Now all I had to pass was the proper driving test.

I knew that my upcoming test wasn't just an examination to see if I could competently and safely control a car. This was going to be very important for my future mobility. It meant the difference between buses, taxis and handicabs forever or being able to go anywhere as and when I pleased. It was that important. And I failed!

The test actually went rather well. I was calm, confident and was doing really well until I inexplicably stopped at a GREEN light in Musselburgh. I didn't cause an accident or anything, but as the examiner had to take verbal action and point out my ridiculous error I automatically failed the test. I was very disappointed with myself and I could tell the examiner had dearly wanted me to pass, but at the end of the day he was only doing his job and I resolved to take the test again as soon as possible. I got a cancellation, and the test was booked for exactly the same time in the morning one month later, November 2004. I booked an extra couple of lessons with Peter and resolved not to make the same, nor indeed any other, mistakes this time.

The next test soon came around and I was even more nervous this time. Knowing what a positive impact that driving would have on my life though I resolved to pass. The way I saw it, I had been through so much shit in the last twenty-two months that a little driving test certainly wasn't going to beat me again. This time I passed and I let out a jubilant 'YEEEEESSS' when the examiner said he was pleased to inform me that I had passed. I had some minor errors but it had basically been a good drive. I think that's the biggest 'YEEEEESSS' I had let out since Tony and I had crossed the border into the Irish Republic in August 2000. This time though I hadn't spoken too soon. I had passed my driving test using intricate hand controls and passed the theory test less than two years after being little more than a charred corpse.

All my family and friends were so pleased for me, both for the practical benefits and the fact that I had achieved it so relatively soon after everything. I was more relieved than anything else but, like remembering Davie's number, cleaning my own teeth, learning to use the manual wheelchair and starting to change my body at the gym, it was another significant step on the road to the almost total recovery I was still determined to make.

I decided not to take advantage of Britain's fantastic Motability scheme until after Christmas as I didn't want to lose any money in the run up to the festive period, which was hopefully going to be my first proper Christmas since 2001. The Motability scheme is an invaluable scheme that allows me to exchange the mobility (help with getting around) component of my disability living allowance care component for a brand new car every three years, as long as I don't go over a certain mileage. I did order my car but asked the dealership if they could wait until after Christmas, which was fine by them as they had to order in my car anyway. Now all I had to worry about was finding around five hundred pounds to have the necessary adaptations carried out on my car. Initially, Motability rejected me for the grant, but I appealed and thankfully they covered the costs for me.

Chapter 41
Assessment

At a meeting with my consultant in Livingston regarding my impending surgery, I got what I thought at the time was bad news. They concluded that the open wound that needed grafting so that I could go back to rehab was no longer suitable to be treated in plastics. For one thing, the wound had grown bigger since my nasty accident at the C.I.S. Cup Final against Livingston that March, and the shard of bone growing out from what was the end of my right 'leg' was still causing problems too. I also still had staples that needed removing from my legs, and I had some tiny fractures in the bone that were also caused by the Hampden incident.

I now needed orthopaedic rather than plastic surgery, to rebuild my leg below the knee, remove the extra shards of bone and the staples and to make my stump more accommodating to prosthesis. I would have to be referred to orthopaedics.

Ever since January 2003 my family had been trying to get me back into St John's. We had been fobbed off with all kinds of excuses and reasons but at this consultation I was told the real reason why I still hadn't been admitted to hospital. The head microbiologist at the hospital simply didn't want me anywhere near the hospital because of the nasty MRSA that I had had when I was in the last time. They wanted three clear swabs from my district nurse showing that I was free from the disease. The fact that I had already been swabbed on several occasions and been found to be free of the bug seemed to matter little, but we went ahead with the new swabs anyway, this being no problem as I still had the district nurse coming in twice a week to dress the open wound on my stump. The wound itself looked horrible as it was easy to see my tibia bone when the wound was undressed. Still, my swabs were clean and I was referred to Dr Macdonald at orthopaedics.

My family, friends and I and even their MP and my GP had been bombarding St John's with letters and emails to get them to get me back in as soon as possible. Mr Butterworth and his team had done a fantastic job of putting me back together again, now it was the turn of orthopaedics to help me get one step closer to walking again. Mr MacDonald, who has a fine reputation, was honest and promised to get me into St John's for the reconstructive orthopaedic surgery in January 2005. Although a full year later than I had initially expected to go back in, I was nevertheless relieved and jubilant to receive this news. Not only was I going to get the open wound that I had had for over a year finally seen too, but after that I would be able to start to use my cool new legs properly again, which had been safely stored at the rehab hospital.

Christmas 2004 loomed. After the disastrous nightmares that had been the previous two Christmases, I was praying for a nice quiet uneventful one, not just for myself, but for my friends and family too. The memory of 2002's evil deed and how sick I had also been at Christmas 2003 played heavy on my heart and mind, and that time of year now always makes me think a lot, thankfully nowadays in a much more positive way. Christmas Day 2004 was spent with my dear, dear friends and their kids, and it was a lovely uneventful but fun and poignant day. That evening I had Tony and Martin round for a while and we had a great laugh, even though we didn't really do much compared to how we used to carry on at weekends and festive times.

Relieved at finally getting a nice Christmas under my belt, I resolved not to push my good luck too far and had a quiet New Year's Eve, partly influenced by the fact that we were playing Hearts on New Year's Day at Easter Road and I wanted to be fresh for that. That game ended in a draw but the atmosphere had been great, even in the West Stand where I still had to sit, for the time being anyway.

Chapter 42
A New Year

I looked forward to 2005 with an optimism that was unparalleled in my life up until that time. I was getting a car in February and was well aware of the massive difference this would make to my life. I was also greatly looking forward to continuing my part time university education as the course I was on, still with the brilliant Dr Chris Brown, which now focused on Scottish military history from our being bullied into union with England in 1707 up until the present day. As that included most of my 'specialist' period (Jacobite Wars in Scotland and Ireland) I couldn't wait to get my teeth into it.

I was also expecting to hear about my claim for criminal injuries compensation in January 2005. I was confident that with the wealth of evidence, the political support I had and after the threats I had received when my Irish girlfriend had gone back home, that I would have my finances secured so as to provide for my future while I looked for a new vocational purpose in life, Baboon-esque warehouse jobs now being, thankfully, a thing of the past. I had applied for around eight hundred thousand pounds from the Irish Criminal Injuries Compensation Authority. The Irish scheme differs from our own UK scheme in that it covers loss of earnings, loss of potential earnings, expenses (both medical and otherwise) but takes no consideration of injuries received or pain and suffering.

Alas, the details of the scheme mattered little as in January 2005 my claim for criminal injuries compensation was rejected, on the grounds that 'It was not clear from the Gardaí report that I had been the victim of a crime'. Obviously my ex had, for some reason, stayed true to her word about being 'ordered' to sabotage my criminal injuries compensation claim and lo and behold my case fell apart after she went home. I've no idea why this happened. I had a Scottish lawyer over there who I had got in contact with through a friend and his help was invaluable to me. However, every letter that he sent to the Gardaí was completely and deliberately ignored, meaning that we never had any real idea of what was going on.

Obviously this was a crushing hammer blow to me and my plans for rebuilding my life, but I was confident that I would be given the compensation I deserved on appeal. Their decision not to pay me out on the basis of it not being clear from the Gardaí report that I was the victim of a crime contradicted everything we had been told thus far. Surely the death threats in 2004 alone were enough to show how sinister the events that Christmas Eve had been, let alone the assault, head wounds, sabotaged door and smoke alarm and illegal non fire retardant furniture, not to mention the suspect apprehended at the scene of the fire by the Gards. As I have mentioned previously, Robin Cook and Jack Straw, MPs, who both did sterling work on my behalf, were told by senior Irish officials that I had been the victim of a hideous crime of violence. The Gards (and I know their names) told my mum face to face early in 2004 that they knew who had done it and how it had been done. Unfortunately, as I said earlier, the only witness to this is my ex and there is no way she will corroborate this now.

This rejection of my just and lawful claim for compensation was a setback, but I had been expecting it since the threats from my ex in the summer of 2004 after she had left. I still, however, had my surgery and rehabilitation proper to begin within a matter of weeks as well as the prospect of getting my new car to look forward to, so I let my family deal with my appeal and the relating correspondence while I focused on the positive stuff.

One thing the late Robin Cook said about the Gardaí in that particular area of Ireland has stayed with me though. He told us that they were one of the most corrupt and incompetent 'police' forces in Europe and that they are often infiltrated by various organisations and some often collude with said organisations, and those Gards who are decent enough and go after the 'big fish' are often intimidated or threatened by the very people they are investigating. In short, for the most part they are glorified security guards, OK for hassling law abiding citizens and chasing kids, but utterly unable or unwilling to pursue real criminals. My own observation after living over there is that the stigma of 'touting' or 'grassing' needs to be eradicated, as their wild and lawless society will never evolve and move on until they de-stigmatise the need to go to the cops about anything.

I may have inadvertently made my claim a little problematic as, when I was hassling the Irish Government and Gardaí via email to do something about my attackers, I foolishly told them that I was aware that my ex's house in Dundalk had been the responsibility of the Health Board, and that I fully intended to pursue a civil claim against them as well as a criminal injuries claim.

This, with hindsight, was silly of me. Now not only did the Irish Government know that I had a large criminal injuries claim in, they also knew that paying me criminal injuries would open the door to a possible multi million pound civil claim against their public sector. I needed the criminal injuries money first, though, as my Scottish lawyer in Ireland would only take on my civil case after I had received my criminal injuries money as, to be blunt, he worked for a small firm and they couldn't risk anything other than a watertight case. Unfortunately, I had no other option as I don't qualify for any 'no win, no fee' aid in the Republic as I'm Scottish. For the same reason I can't get a lawyer over here to take it as it is out of the jurisdiction of Scottish law.

The Scottish parliament I now see as little more than a glorified county council, such has been their impotence in trying to help me. For an organisation that works co closely with the Irish parliament, it's disheartening the amount of 'not my problem, can't do anything' replies I've had from various so-called 'big wigs' at Holyrood. Ultimately though, the blame lies with the Gards, my attackers and those within the Irish Government who obviously don't give a fuck what happened to an insignificant 'Brit' who's only mistake was to move to a dodgy town he knew nothing about. Why would they want to pay such a 'Brit' compensation from their economy? (I'm Scottish by the way, not British. Being British is a state of mind.)

In any case, with the full support of Robin Cook and Jack Straw we put in an appeal, though by now I was going to class anything that I received from the CICA as a bonus. Perversely, they even rejected my mum's claim to have her expenses covered, as they had been incurred due to a crime, despite it being usual policy to do so (my mum was on benefits at the time). That really was sick. Their cops swear to my mum's face that they knew who tried to kill her son, then eventually they won't even pay her expenses via compensation.

Chapter 43
Under The Knife Again

Having my claim rejected made me very angry, to say the least. However it wasn't the end of the world and I still had positive things to look forward to.

The date I was given for my surgery was 1 February 2005, and I was to be admitted in ward 14 at St John's. I was actually excited about going back into hospital and getting on with my life. The operation didn't scare me at all. I just wanted to get cracking. In any case, I had complete faith in Mr Macdonald and his team. This time when I went back into hospital I knew what to expect.

I went in on the actual morning of my operation and resolved to myself that from here on I would focus only on the positive in life. It seems strange now to have had such an adrenalin rush about something like a major operation, but that's what it was like. I initially got a fright when I woke up in recovery after the procedure as I was struggling to stay awake, but my mum was there and I had good wishes passed to me via messages from family and friends. That unmistakable feeling of an anaesthetic hangover was scary at first, and it reminded be briefly of those dark days in Dublin fighting for my life.

That feeling didn't last long however, and after a night's brilliant aftercare recovering on the ward, I had managed to eat with no problem and was busily texting my friends and preparing to watch the League Cup semi-final in my hospital room, a clash between Dundee Utd and Rangers. That brought back memories of that amazing victory over Rangers we had had at the same stage of the competition in 2004, exactly one year previously. Unfortunately, Dundee Utd played like eleven clowns with pineapples shoved up their behinds and were crushed 7-1 by Rangers, who went on to win the cup, thumping Motherwell 5-1 in the final.

Within a few days it was clear that my operation to rebuild my right leg below my knee had been a complete success, though I thought my leg below the knee now looked like a giant sausage. I actually became a bit of an annoying patient after a few days. I had the operation on the Monday but was completely recovered, if not healed, by the Wednesday.

Burnt

I wanted to go home. I would have got a taxi home if need be as ambulance transport might have taken time to arrange. In the end my brilliant consultant, Mr Macdonald, saw how fit and well I looked, how keen I was to get home and above all that my leg seemed to be in great shape. I was allowed to go home on the Thursday, less than three whole days after my operation. I was to come back to hospital every couple of weeks to have my healing checked and to have my stitches out but I was happy with that. I really felt like things were starting to turn the corner for me now, recovery wise.

I remember my mum stayed with me that Thursday night and we watched the movie 'Troy' together, and thoroughly enjoyed it. I remember remarking at how realistic the amputees in the battle scenes looked.

Chapter 44
Driving

Soon after my operation I picked up my brand new car from my local dealership. I felt so nervous when I was given the keys and basically told, 'It's yours now, drive it home.' I managed to get it home safely, through rush hour, too. At first getting in and out of my car was hard as I not only had to transfer from my wheelchair into the driver's seat, but I also had to dismantle the chair, fold it up and throw it back across my body in to the back seat. This was tough at first but I soon got used to it. Driving has changed my life forever as it has given me a freedom of movement that is invaluable and has allowed me to do the things I now do every day. It has also greatly helped my social life to recover as I can now meet friends or family anytime without having to rely on lifts or expensive taxis.

I loved my black automatic car. The single thing I like most about driving is that when I'm out on the road it's like I'm not disabled. I'm just as fast and mobile as everyone else on the road and it feels great.

In 2004 Hibs installed a new manager in ex Celtic defender Tony Mowbray. I actually applied for the job myself, citing my experiences of managing Hibs in computer games as good reasons for employing me. Unsurprisingly my tongue in cheek application was turned down, though the club did at least write back with a 'Thanks, but no thanks' response, which gave me and the lads a giggle. In the end, employing Tony Mowbray rather than me proved to be the right decision. Mowbray's appointment along with the superlative performances of our multitude of exciting young players soon saw us transferred from bottom six into UEFA Cup challengers. Watching this exciting, brilliant football from 2004 until the present day has been extremely helpful in my recovery and rehabilitation. This wasn't the only thing that helped me though.

I had been suffering from posttraumatic stress and flashbacks ever since the incident, but this had got much worse after the threats I received about dropping the case. I was referred to the Rivers Centre in Edinburgh to receive counselling and to discuss what, if any, medication was needed to combat this condition.

The counselling itself seemed pretty bog standard, though I was lucky to have a very understanding and kind counsellor called Kathleen. We spent a lot of sessions talking through things, as you would expect. Sometimes it is easier to talk to a stranger about how you feel and what you are experiencing and in this case it really helped. She taught me a few neat mental tricks to use to block out unpleasant flashbacks and even taught me an invaluable method for neutralising the effects of horrid nightmares about the fire incident. Basically, whenever I have one of these awful repeat nightmares, I imagine myself to be in my old room at St John's in Livingston as this was the first place since the fire where I had felt safe. It works too.

She concluded that considering the attempted murder thing, being made severely disabled for life, not being able to work, being thrown back into the mix with my family again (a good thing), not having much money and having my initial claim for criminal injuries compensation rejected, that I had done exceptionally well.

She didn't think I needed any further counselling, and I agreed. We discussed long-term medication, but to be honest all the drugs I was offered for my nightmares either make you put on weight or make you impotent, neither of which I was willing to risk. The nightmares are getting less and less all the time.

Chapter 45
Bigots

Hibs predictably ruined my 27th birthday by losing yet another Scottish Cup semi-final to Dundee Utd at Hampden, despite leading 1-0 thanks to a Derek Riordan penalty. I went to this game with my dad, with whom I am glad to say I have sorted everything out. Typically though, Hibs threw away yet another chance to win the cup by losing to a very average Dundee Utd side that went on to lose the final to Celtic anyway.

Unfortunately it won't be the football I'll remember this game for. There was a minute's silence for Pope John Paul II at this match but it was ruined by one arsehole Hibs fan who shouted 'Fuck the pope'. I was so angry. Not only as a Catholic, not only as a devoted fan whose team's heritage is Irish and Catholic, but also as a human being. Anyone who can't keep their mouth shut for one minute out of respect for someone who has died is vermin in my book.

Thankfully this was overshadowed in the media by the other semi-final the next day between Hearts and Celtic. Almost the entire Hearts support booed the minute's silence so that it had to be abandoned. The excuses offered by Hearts fans for this included, 'Ah but the Catholic Church and child abuse' or 'What's the Pope got to do with football?' which were painfully transparent attempts to disguise their inherent bigotry. I know a lot of decent Hearts supporters who were disgusted by this episode. Thankfully, justice was done and Celtic easily beat Hearts to reach the final. And just to rub salt in Hearts' wounds, they had a ten minute chorus of 'Dirty orange bastards' from the Celtic fans after the minute's silence, followed by the whole Celtic rebel song repertoire as their team lamely surrendered to Celtic.

This incident, and what went the day before would have had me foaming at the mouth with rage only a few years before. Now, after everything that has happened, it only made me sad and reminded me of one of the reasons I had left Scotland in the first place. Still, it seems the law and the Scottish Football Association are finally doing something about this blight on

Scottish society and hopefully our future generations will grow up in a land without such bigotry.

Hibs eventually finished third in 2005 which was a remarkable achievement, although it was in somewhat bittersweet circumstances after our lame surrender to Rangers on the last day of the season at Easter Road, Rangers winning the league on 'our patch' as it were.

In the early part of 2005 my friends and I spent a lot of time helping out my friend Martin, who was being harassed by some rat bully from West Lothian. I might have had no legs, but believe you me if I could have gotten hold of this sicko I don't know what might have happened. In the end I was angrier about this scumbag hassling Martin than I was about my own ongoing case. Martin is not the fighting type and therefore anyone who hits this type of person is a bully and a coward.

Martin wisely told the police about this scumbag and, surprise surprise, we found out that the scumbag in question had done this before. It was great the way all of our friends and Martin's brother Paul got together to sort this mess out, and we didn't even have to resort to violence. Like the true coward that he was, the bully caved in after a few 'straight talking' phone calls from friends of mine, and from lots of random weirdos after his number was posted in a sleazy Internet chat room.

Chapter 46
Get Cracking

I didn't have much time to reflect on the end of the football season as I was soon invited to see my prosthetist, Francine, to try out my legs again. Though it felt great to be upright it was clear that I needed extensive physiotherapy. I could get physio at Astley Ainslie as an outpatient but my time would be limited and I wouldn't receive as much physio as I would as an in-patient.

At first I baulked at the idea of going back into hospital. I couldn't face going back into Astley Ainslie, not because there was anything wrong with the place or the staff, as there wasn't, it was just the memories of 2003 when I was all wounds and nasty scars. I had a couple of outpatient appointments with the brilliant Catriona and Rona, the physios, but we soon agreed that I needed the kind of intensive physio that I could only really get if I went back to Astley Ainslie as an in-patient. However, things were different now. I had a car, which meant I was in no way stuck in the hospital, and I could of course go home at the weekends when there was no physio. I agreed with the physios and they set about arranging for me to get back into the ward.

In the meantime I just loved having my car. I could go anywhere I wanted to, whenever I wanted to. It was so liberating. The gym had made a big difference to me. I now had big powerful arms and shoulders and my chest was getting stronger. This fitness was to prove crucial in my forthcoming rehab.

In January I had attended part two of my military history course. I found this course to be even more interesting and stimulating and I was surprised when I was asked to stay behind after the lecture one evening. Chris, the lecturer, said that the essay that I had handed in for the last block was first class, and that I obviously had a talent for understanding and writing about this topic. I was flabbergasted, but at the same time was immensely proud. He went on to tell me that with my wealth of knowledge and understanding it would be a little pointless in me doing a bog standard BA or MA in history unless I wanted to be a civil servant or a school teacher, and that my wealth of knowledge on the subject might actually work against me doing one of these two degrees. He suggested that I should go straight to PhD level. It's not impossible to do that, and I could get accepted to do the PhD on the strength of what I had written thus far.

This was a great boost to my morale. I had started these courses just for therapeutic reasons, yet here a celebrated academic was telling me that I was good enough to do a PhD. Not bad for someone who hadn't been in a classroom since high school. I was further elated when I received an 'A' for the exam at the end of the second part of the course. I had written a top-notch essay about the decline of the edged weapon in the military in the latter seventeenth/early eighteenth century, a far cry from humping boxes of food around in warehouses, and a world away from fighting for my life with 65% burns in a foreign land.

Upon this tutor's advice I approached my director of studies. Edinburgh has no War Studies department, so unfortunately I would have to go to Glasgow or St Andrews. This presented me with quite a few logistical problems so I opted instead to apply to do a run of the mill MA in Scottish History at Edinburgh.

That was quite a long way off though and, as you'll remember, I had the small matter of learning to walk again to take care of first…

Chapter 47
Here We Go

I went back into Sutherland ward of the Astley Ainslie Hospital early in June 2005. There was no specific timescale on my stay, I was essentially there until I could walk again.

It was strange being back there under such different circumstances to those that I had arrived under in 2003. This time I shared a room with a man a little older than me called Geoff, who was actually from the same old estate as me in Livingston. In fact, he only lived a few doors along from my mate Davie. I enjoyed sharing a room as opposed to being in isolation this time, as I was by now a lot more comfortable with talking about things than I was first time around.

I was also lucky in that all the lovely staff from when I was in first time around were still there. I was basically only there for physiotherapy so I often came home for a couple of hours in the evening so I could play Rocky on my Xbox or watch Sky TV.

Physio started off somewhat intensely, which suited me just fine. By now I hadn't walked in just over two and a half years. My transverse abdominus and other balance related muscles were very weak, despite the little exercises I had been persevering with during the interim between my last stay in hospital. I had lost a lot of weight since starting to go to the gym regularly in 2004 but was still carrying too much around my midriff, and that was an area that only walking would be of use for in fighting the flab. I was, though, as fit as I could possibly have been for the Herculean task that lay ahead. Now it was up to me, the physios and God. The leg that had been operated on in February had healed brilliantly, though obviously I still had niggling doubts about its strength after what happened before.

First things first. I wheeled myself over to the parallel bars and started to put on my prosthetic legs. First my above knee left limb. I rolled on the silicon sock so that it covered the scarred but smooth stump tightly, then pulled a thin white cloth sock and then a thick terry towelling sock on over that. The silicon sock had a little threaded part on the end that my actual leg would eventually screw on to, while the cloth and woollen socks had holes in the end so that they didn't interfere with the part on the end. This whole process takes a minute or two.

Then it was time to put on my right leg, the below knee one, the one that had caused me so much trouble. I started by rolling on the TEC silicon liner, taking care to ensure that no air pockets were trapped inside that might put me off balance. Then, I pulled a long silk sock over the liner that came up to round about my right mid thigh, stretching it tight. I finished off this bizarre ensemble with another terry towelling sock pulled over the silk one. Then all I had to do was pull the airtight sleeve attached to my right leg up over my knee. The sleeve is the same colour as support tights, which I found mildly amusing. Next I took the length of string from inside my left prosthesis and screwed the little cap onto the threads at the end of my left liner. When I had screwed it in tight enough I pulled the chord at the side of my leg until I heard it 'click'. The physios, Joan and Rona, watched as I steadied myself to do something that I hadn't done properly in two-and-a-half years. I was about to stand up straight.

The left (above knee) leg that I have has a fixed rather than a moving knee to give me extra stability. When I get upright it locks, giving me a very stable but straight leg. But I had to get up there first. Using the enormous strength that the gym and pushing my wheelchair had given me, I pushed up on the end of the parallel bars until I was up straight enough to lock my knee. I started to sweat buckets almost the instant that I got up there, but that mattered little. Ian Colquhoun was standing up!

It didn't stop there. Using the parallel bars and my arms for extra stability, I started to walk the length of the bars. It felt so strange but I was finally doing it. When I reached the other end of the bars the sweat running down my face turned partly to tears, such was my happiness. I was walking!

When I turned around to go back the mere ten or fifteen paces that I had just covered I received a spontaneous round of applause from all the other amputees in the gym and from the physiotherapy staff. I felt a pride burning in my heart that I had never experienced before, but at the same time a gratitude and humility regarding what I had achieved that made me thank God over and over again in my head. All my worries about my newly rebuilt leg simply evaporated as I managed not one, not two, not four, but eight lengths of the parallel bars! After this feat I collapsed back into my wheelchair, puffing and panting and aching all over, but at the same time feeling overwhelmed with joy. I drank a cup of water given to me by the physiotherapy assistant and was told by my brilliant physios that I had done enough for one morning and could go back to the ward for a welcome break.

I sat in my wheelchair and zoomed across to the ward as fast as I could so that I could check my leg for anything untoward. Slowly, nervously, I peeled off the liners and looked. Nothing. It had held up! Grinning from ear to ear I proceeded to phone and text my friends and family one by one to tell them my good news.

I ate a hearty lunch on the ward, knowing I would need the energy, and then headed back across to physio for round two in the afternoon. That afternoon I started off on the parallel bars again, and even got someone to video me doing it so that I could send the clip around everyone I knew. The clip of me in my shorts wearing my FC St Pauli top struggling along those parallel bars was soon doing the rounds with all the people who mattered to me. I even watched it myself a few times later on, just a few hundred.

I was shocked but nevertheless undeterred when my physiotherapist then handed me a pair of elbow crutches. It seemed daunting at first but I was keen to try them at least once. Supervised closely by Joan, I took the crutches and started to walk slowly along the gym. I barely managed one length as crutches take a lot more energy to use than parallel bars, and I was soon sitting down again, panting and sweating. Nevertheless, for the briefest of moments I had been upright on crutches and walked across the room. I was getting there, but very slowly. That night I slept better than I had in months, though I'm sure my snoring must have kept my ward mate Geoff awake!

I met a lot of fabulous people that second time in Astley Ainslie. I'll spare the blushes of the gorgeous trainee physio whom I sent flowers too just for being so nice to me. I met a lot of inspirational men and women who had all lost limbs under different circumstances and we often exchanged advice and tips. While in there I met a girl called Louise who had suffered even more horrific injuries than me. We became good pals and, to be honest, her positive attitude and personality helped inspire me to keep trying.

Physio got a tiny bit easier every day. I would start off with a few lengths of the parallel bars to warm up, making sure I kept my abdominal muscles contracted so that it would strengthen my balance. Then I would move onto crutches, though the first few times I could barely manage one or two lengths of the gym on them. It was exhausting. Utterly exhausting! I literally had sweat streaming down my face like tears and my arms kept aching, but they never gave way, thanks to all the work I had done in the gym. I don't think I would have walked a step again if it hadn't been for the gym.

The physiotherapists hit on a masterstroke when they suggested that I practice my walking with them out in the big long corridor that ran the length of the physiotherapy block. This had two main effects. Firstly, it removed my self-consciousness about sweating so much in front of everyone and exposed me to a mild, cooling breeze. Secondly, it gave me a much bigger distance to potentially walk along, and all in one straight line. It wasn't the walking that was the toughest part though. It was getting from sit to stand. With only one working knee I simply couldn't get upright out of my chair without using the bars or a radiator to grab onto and use as leverage so I could get up straight enough to lock my left fixed knee. We agreed to focus on my sit to stand for a few days, though we kept walking along the corridor too.

My physios were very encouraging to me, using the right balance of praise and good old fashioned 'get on with it' when needed. And it was to work a treat. Sometimes I would do nothing in a session other than sit to stand, and sometimes it was so hard to wrench myself out of the chair that those tears would make the odd appearance, though these were tears of determination rather than tears of despair. It was tough going.

All the extra effort was making me sleep like the proverbial top at night and it had also given me a voracious appetite. Just as well really, as I needed every last kilo joule of energy that my body could provide. This time I didn't find the hospital food revolting, I found it energising. This time I didn't wake up in tears when I remembered where I was, instead I would wake up eager to get cracking with the day's physio.

I decided after some advice that I needed to practice as much as possible at remaining upright to improve my balance. This didn't necessarily mean walking. Then my physio Katrina came up with another masterstroke. She got me to kneel on a gym bed with my arms flat out holding onto a massive red gym ball. All I had to do was keep myself upright on my makeshift knees for as long as possible and rotate my hips now and then. This was by far the hardest exercise I could do, but I felt the benefits almost instantaneously and this spurred me on to do it even more. Day after day, session after session, I would just work with the gym ball, strengthening my transverse abdominus and getting my body more and more used to being upright. Sometimes it was agony but I never allowed the pain impulses going to my brain to override my burning desire to walk again and, slowly but surely, I felt my balance muscles getting stronger and stronger.

After a couple of weeks of this, with me going home to relax at the weekends, I was getting slightly better at walking. Every time my two physios and I went out to the corridor I would walk a little further than the last time, not much, but a little, and these gradual increases inspired me to try that little bit harder every day. With the encouragement of my physios, I soon had the hang of the as yet very difficult sit to stand method, and I was even doing a little bit of walking back on the ward between sessions just to keep my muscles ticking over. I was cracking it! I was walking again, almost.

I got the fright of my life one afternoon when my knee started to throb after I had collapsed in my usual sweating, breathless heap after a walk along the corridor. With every step I took my knee was getting sorer. It eventually got so bad that I could barely get ten yards without having to stop from the pain. I was terrified that my knee was going to pack in and stop me from walking again. I prayed that it would not, surely not after coming this far.

My physios saw how concerned I was and looked into the problem, and told me what it was. The problem was my knee. Remember I told you that I have a kind of artificially made composite knee made up of what was left of my own right knee and the bits of my calf muscle that hadn't been burned in the fire. It wasn't designed or, rather, it wasn't capable of bearing my weight when my leg was in full extension. Put simply, my knee was jamming, hyper extended with every step I took. I knew from the look on my physio's face that the solution wasn't going to be surgery and I was even more relieved when she showed me what the solution was. It was a simple orthotic knee brace, like those worn by injured sportsmen when recovering. It wasn't exactly in my favourite colour, being royal blue, but that didn't really matter.

Almost as soon as I put it on I could feel a difference and I was soon back to walking decent lengths of the corridor again. I had been terrified that a dodgy knee might ruin my chances of walking again or, worse still, that it might be infected and need amputating. I had nothing to fear though, and the simple addition of this basic but hugely effective knee brace allowed me to carry on where I had left off.

Next I was taken through to the stairs. At first the stairs looked daunting, a step too far, possibly because I had grown so used seeing steps in my wheelchair and knowing that I couldn't get up them. My physios reassured me that it WAS possible and that I could do it. Sure enough, I fought back my fear and started to climb the practice flight of about ten steps. They were fairly steep and the first few times I went up and down them I became the now familiar panting, sweating wreck. By now though it was taking longer and longer for me to get so tired. It was while climbing these stairs that I felt I had turned the corner in learning to walk again.

I had just successfully managed the stairs for the umpteenth time that afternoon when it dawned on me. These steps were about the same steepness as the steps that led onto the East Stand at Easter Road, the stand I had last been on at that Aberdeen game in 2002, the stand that I had been effectively barred from because of my wheelchair, and the stand that I longed to get back to so that I could watch Hibs the way that I used to, the way it should be.

Realising that I was now fit enough and able to walk back onto the terracing galvanised me to keep practising until I was perfect at it. Soon there was no stopping me. My physios had me going up and down the corridor, going over obstacles in the gym, standing on balance platforms and going up and down ramps. I had cracked it! Only one in five double amputees can walk at all yet here I was, after less than five weeks of intensive physiotherapy, able to walk with two elbow crutches! I had done it!

I was so eager to get out of hospital and start showing everyone my legs that I basically did a runner from the hospital on the Thursday night, forgetting to take my discharge medication. The staff at Astley Ainslie all looked so pleased to see me walking, and Dr Hutton, the ward specialist, had said that my physiotherapy had more or less finished, so no one minded me leaving. The feeling that I had after putting my legs in the back of the car and driving home was one that will stay with me forever.

Chapter 48
Homeward Bound

When I got home my mum and her friend Marilyn were in my house doing some of the housework that I can't do and I saw tears of joy well up in my mum's eyes when she saw me get up out of the wheelchair and walk around the house. Marilyn had a digital camcorder so another little impromptu video of my walking was made. I felt so proud showing them that I could walk again.

Next I decided to go in to Livingston to show off my new legs to my friends and family. My mates Davie and Jenny and their two kids looked overjoyed to see me up and about wearing trousers, something that they hadn't seen since they came to see me in Dundalk in September 2002. Their wee boy Marc grinned from ear to ear when he saw me walking and their daughter Kerry even had a wee smile for me, though she looked a little puzzled at seeing me upright!

My friends Martin and Tony were equally impressed and looked really happy to see me finally walking after so long. I also went and showed my sister Angela who, again, was delighted and inspired to see me walking again. It must have been great for my dad to finally see his son stand tall again when I went up to see him and his wife Susan. The fact that I had actually lost an inch and was now only six feet tall was only noticed by me. I got similarly warm reactions from my pals Maggie and John and their family when they saw me walking.

Everyone just seemed so pleased for me and I just wanted to show them that I could do it. I had battled attempted murder, arson, life threatening burns, kidney failure, multiple operations, MRSA, coma and the stigma of not getting back into hospital because of a bug that I had carried. I had went from being little more than a charred, blistered corpse on Christmas morning 2002 to almost being what I would class as a normal guy again. It had taken me two-and-a-half years to get this far. Ian Colquhoun was back. But I still had some work to do…

Burnt

In September 2005 I was asked to give a lecture to physiotherapy students at Edinburgh's Queen Margaret College. This seemed daunting at first but I wanted to do my bit to help these students understand how to deal with amputees. I was doubled up with my friend Olivia and we spoke extensively to two different groups of students, showing them our limbs and advising them on how to treat amputees. We then had a question and answer session with them and it was rounded off by them giving Olivia and I a round of applause. It was a good day, I felt that I had done something to help future amputees and it was great to see Olivia again. I hope they ask me to do it again.

Though I now had my new legs and could wear them and use them reasonably well, I still had quite a lot to learn about using them. Stairs and slopes were the biggest hazard to me. I negotiated stairs by going up them leading with my right leg, the one with the knee, then easing my fixed left leg up after it. Coming down stairs you do the opposite. You put the fixed left leg down first to give you stability and then you put the right one down. In both cases you have to grab the stair banister with one hand while using an elbow crutch with the other. This could be tricky as this meant I had to get whoever was with me to carry the spare crutch while I climbed or descended the stairs, or if I was alone I had to carefully hook one crutch over my forearm so that I didn't trip over it.

It's basically the same with slopes and ramps. Lead with the left leg when going down, lead with the right when going up. The steeper the slope, the bigger the effort.

Getting used to getting in and out of my car wearing my legs was at first a challenge, but I eventually cracked it. I simply open the driver's door and face away from the seat, plonking my bottom on it and then unlocking and bending my left leg so that I can swing around to face the steering wheel. It took some perfecting at first, but I can do it easily now.

I rarely wear my legs at home in the house. There are two reasons for this. Firstly, most things in my house are at wheelchair height, like they were in my last place, so it's easier to do things around the house in my wheelchair. Secondly, walking with two fake legs means that I use around six times the energy that an able bodied person uses to do the same things. This, together with the fact that I like to minimise the risk of wear and tear on my stump, means that I take my legs off at home to give myself and my stumps a well-earned rest.

Living on my own as I do at the moment there are certain household tasks that I myself simply cannot do, either in my chair or on my limbs. Things like changing my bed, sweeping the front and back paths, mopping the floors, hoovering and laundry are all a little difficult for me, though I can manage everything else. I'm lucky in that I get help with those tasks from my mum, her friend Dorothy and sometimes from my pal Maggie. Cooking isn't an issue as I am, and always have been, an amazing cook, when I can be bothered.

The reaction I got from others when I started going around on my legs was very positive. The people at my local gym were delighted for me, and a little amazed, which is understandable as they had only ever seen me in my wheelchair, legless, as it were. It must have been a positive experience to the gym staff too, seeing the difference that their help and encouragement had made, not only to my appearance, but also to my life in general.

The same can be said of my lecturer and university staff. They all looked pleased to see me up and about. One of my courses was held in Edinburgh Castle for a time and the cobbled stones and steep steps there were a great but tough challenge for me so soon after getting my new legs. I managed them fine, though I was exhausted after every class.

In August 2005 I was asked to appear in a national newspaper giving an account of what had happened to me. I needed the money and felt that my story might help others who have suffered burns or amputations, so I agreed to do it.

The lovely reporter wrote the story respectfully and tastefully and I even got to wear my Hibs top in the photo shoot! The story focused mainly on my MRSA thing and on how I had finally been fitted with new limbs. Thankfully the kind journalist wasn't interested in the nasty side of what had happened and, to be honest, I didn't want to talk much about that anyway, so I was pleased with the article, though I did look awfully fat in the photos. Still, better to be fat than to have no legs! I got five or six hundred pounds for this story, and another five hundred pounds from a magazine that the journalist set me up with. The magazine wasn't my cup of tea and I haven't seen it but by all accounts it was a good article.

Burnt

After I was in the paper I had the maddest couple of days that I had had in a long time. I was inundated with texts, calls and mail from people whom I hadn't seen for ages, all wishing me their best and asking me if I was OK. Strangers who had seen the features stopped me in the street on numerous occasions and even they wanted to wish me well. Even the brilliant people from my Hibs fans forum offered me messages of support and encouragement. Doing the newspaper article helped me bury a few ghosts about what had happened, in a similar way to how writing this book is helping me.

Chapter 49
New Season

The football season came and I, of course, finally got myself a season ticket for the East Stand at Easter Road. Though I was on the East Stand at a couple of games when the season started, it didn't really hit home until we played local rivals Hearts at Easter Road that October.

Hearts had recently been taken over by a Lithuanian businessman and he had signed lots of good players and installed the brilliant George Burley as their manager. They had already beaten us 4-0 in the first derby of the season at Tynecastle and had since been undefeated and were top of the league, their only black spot being a humiliating League Cup exit to crappy Livingston. Thankfully, by the time they came to play us their Lithuanian chairman had hounded out Burley in probably the worst decision in Hearts' history. With Burley gone, so too were their chances of being champions. But this was a derby game. League positions mattered little.

As we approached Easter Road we could hear Hearts fans singing 'we are unbeatable, we are unbeatable' to an old Italian tune. I managed to squeeze myself and my crutches through the tight turnstile and then proceeded to climb the steep steps that take you onto the East Stand, or the terracing, as we call it. It was a hard slog up the steps but the buzz I got when I crested the top of the steps and saw the nearly full ground filling with supporters almost brought a tear to my eye. It felt like I had come home. It may have been a peculiar target to focus on for major rehabilitation, but all those months of waiting and all the painful and exhausting physiotherapy had been worth it. I took my seat. I had to sit in the front row as I couldn't stand up easily but that didn't matter. I was finally back on the East Stand! Surely it couldn't get any better than this? It did!

We sang our heads off for the whole game and humbled the 'unbeatable' Hearts 2-0, with goals from Garry O'Connor and Guilleium Beuzelin.

Burnt

We even rubbed in our victory by singing Hearts' own song back at them, changing the lyrics to 'you're not unbeatable, you're not unbeatable'. It was great to be back in amongst the more vocal element of our support where I belonged, and even better to beat our local rivals. They were to get the better of us that season on the whole. They won their two home derby games, we won our two, but Hearts defeated our injury-ravaged team 4-0 in the cup semi-final at Hampden, ruining my birthday a little once again. But it was worth it for me. My first derby being able to walk and being on the East Stand again was a personal victory that I will cherish forever.

By now I was losing weight all the time thanks to the walking and my regular visits to the gym. I went from a forty-inch waist to a thirty-six inch in little more than three weeks. I could start wearing nice clothes again rather than sportswear, which was a relief. I never liked having to wear tracksuits and stuff when I was in the wheelchair as I've always been well dressed. Now I could go clothes shopping at proper shops again. I'm now a thirty-two inch waist again, the same size I was before all that shit happened.

My body has changed a lot too. When I was first discharged from hospital I had man boobs and saggy flabby arms, but I have now changed them into big solid pecs with powerful muscular arms and shoulders. My facial scarring is almost gone and the scars on the rest of my body are healing nicely. My weight loss isn't just down to the gym and walking. I made subtle changes to my diet too. Sweeteners instead of sugar, semi-skimmed instead of full fat milk and eating more fruit and vegetables than I have ever done before have all made the difference in changing the way I look. I'm still a big laddie, but one thing I'm definitely not now is fat.

I was by now also spending the weekends with my friends again. I would either visit the ones in Livingston or have Martin up here to have a couple of beers and watch silly comedy, which is always a laugh with him. I had also started to get on brilliantly with the neighbours, chiefly Rab, Mark and Samantha, who are brilliant people. It was a tough decision to eventually move house early in 2006 as I knew I would miss them, but I'm a still firm friend with them.

That September we all went out to Room at the Top in Bathgate. I took my car and my gorgeous new girlfriend Janie along and we had a great night, although it understandably wasn't the same as it used to be when I could dance. Up until that night I had been almost afraid of listening to dance music as it reminded me of the fact that I couldn't dance to it any more.

Something happened that night to change that though, and although I listen to a wide selection of music now (some of which would no doubt make you cringe), dance music is once again my favourite, whether out and about, in a pub or club or in the car. The album 'One Love' by Uniting Nations, which I think is the best British dance album since Faithless, I find particularly groovy and uplifting. It's a bit cheesy but I prefer that now to the pretentious crap that no one has ever heard before. And you'll never guess who I recently found out is part of this dance act. The same guy who did the 'Kung Fu Fighting' cover in 1998 that I heard over and over in my coma! Spooky or what?

I had the first of only three falls to date that night in Bathgate, though thankfully I was able to steady myself on Janie and a handy pillar. That one wasn't even my fault. The floor was wet. My other falls since were one just outside my house when it was raining, a fall which didn't hurt me but gave me a fright all the same, and a quite silly one on my birthday in 2006. I was out clubbing with all my friends and when I tried to get up off the tall stool I was sitting on I didn't lock my knee properly and I ended up falling down. Thankfully, the kind bouncers at 'Cav' and my friends all made sure I was OK, and the only damage I sustained was a tiny cut to my knee.

Christmas and New Year 2005 were an absolute scream. At Christmas we had a lads' night out down at our local pub then a party afterwards. I went out in my wheelchair so that I didn't have to worry about falling and we had an awesome time out together. On the way home we even played a prank. The street beside the pub had only recently re-opened to traffic after extensive road works but the road works materials like the cones, signs and barriers were still stacked neatly at the side of the road. We put all the road works back exactly the way that they had been and pissed ourselves with laughter before all heading down the road roaring a slightly inappropriate song about then Hearts player Rudi Skacel. We were all absolutely hammered. The road remained 'closed' for two days until someone noticed what was going on and called the council.

New Year saw us mostly all together again at Maggie and John's for a party. Their parties were legendary. That too was a great night, at which I spent most of the night playing DJ on their PC. Everyone kept asking for 'Proximus' by Mauro Picotto and it must have been played at least eight times. Sometimes the parties there were just as good as being at a club.

Chapter 50
Guess What?

January 2006 initially brought bad news. Surprise surprise, my criminal injuries appeal had been rejected and it seemed the Gardaí had completely changed their tune about what had happened. I was expecting it though, but I thought it was peculiar that they waited until bang on three years before rejecting my claim for compensation. The three years being up, I was now unable to make a civil claim even if I had been able to find someone to take it on.

It's a bitter pill to swallow knowing that no one is being jailed for what happened to me, but not being compensated just takes the biscuit. It simply isn't fair. I wasn't helped when Robin Cook died, but his successor Jim Devine did the best he could. I thank these two men, and the kind Scottish lawyer in Ireland who helped me free of charge, despite the Gardaí ignoring all the letters he sent. When I phoned him after receiving this bad news he was honest and told me it was because of the Gardaí. But we had all already figured that out long ago.

I still have an open appeal which I would have to attend in person for criminal injuries, but I won't be wasting the money on the plane ticket. I don't trust the Gardaí or the Criminal Injuries Compensation Authority and I know now that they just don't want to pay out to a foreigner. I've since met a few people who have had similar seemingly cut and dried criminal injuries cases in the Irish Republic knocked back, and they blame the Gardaí too. They aren't like our own police, unfortunately.

I continued at university in 2006, starting off with early modern Europe and a counselling and psychotherapy course, as the uni had insisted that I do some non-history topics. The history course was OK, and I met some lovely people on both courses, which were taught by interesting lecturers, but the counselling and psychotherapy one was tedious. I almost fell asleep a few times. I'm slightly historically biased in my support for the Stuarts and this

Burnt

affected my grade for the European history course, though nothing I actually said was wrong. I wrote a complete mockery of an essay for the counselling course but to my amazement still passed!

Chapter 51
Stump Idol

I saw an advert in 2005 looking for people who wanted help from scientists for a new Channel 4 TV show called 'Men In White'. I applied to go on it and asked them to 'jazz up' my brilliant but plain prosthetic legs. The lovely producer Rachel was soon in touch and I agreed to go on the program. They arranged for my mum and I to fly to London and stay in a hotel right next to the new Wembley Stadium so that I could try out these add ons for my legs in the studio. The film crew first came and filmed me in my old flat and in the pub near where I used to live with a couple of my mates.

The trip to London was great. I love London and while the team from the program were 'jazzing up' my legs I managed to go out sightseeing with my mum for the day. The highlight was going on the London Eye with my mum. It took a little gentle persuasion to get her to go on it, as she normally doesn't like heights, but we did and both thought it was fantastic. I even had my Hibs top on so I just had to buy the extortionate photo of us high over the London skyline in our 'pod'. That was a great day.

When we went back to the studio my leg part was nearly ready. The program, 'Men in White', is about three genius scientists from different specialist areas working together to solve problems or appeals for help sent in by viewers. Their work includes a floating bicycle, a car that can't be towed away or clamped and a silent hair drier. Their task for me was simple. Pimp my leg. And they certainly did. They made me an attachment that clips onto the pole on my left leg between the 'knee' and the foot. They couldn't interfere with my actual legs as I have my particular type of limbs for specific medical reasons, but they made me an awesome 'add on'. It was basically a lightweight metal unit held onto my leg pole by an Allen key. The unit features a docking system for an MP3 player and speakers, a point for plugging in my mobile phone so that I can answer it via a proper phone handset stored inside, an alarm, a set of funky disco lights and a working pedometer. Inspector Gadget indeed! Or the bionic man!

Burnt

I actually quite enjoyed being on camera and all the people at Tiger Aspect, the company who were making the show for Channel 4, were first class, from the runners right through to the scientists and producer. To be honest I quite fancied the producer, Rachel, but I'm sure she won't mind me telling you that.

When I got back from London I moved into my new house and settled in quickly. I carried on with my studies and my next two courses were social sciences, again at the insistence of the university, and a course on my 'specialist' subject, the Jacobites, with the brilliant Stuart McHardy MA.

I met some great people on the social sciences course but, again, as it was non-history it was about as interesting as watching paint dry. So again I wrote another piss take essay for that course and guess what! I passed it again, though I was reprimanded for writing 'an attack on right wing politics'.

The Jacobites course was great and I enjoyed debating with people who actually knew what they were talking about. The lecturer, Stuart McHardy, was also very helpful to me, with encouragement and advice on what I should do next.

I've now decided to abandon my MA for a number of reasons. Firstly, a third of the course is non-history so that would lessen my enthusiasm for study greatly. Secondly, my extensive knowledge of certain periods might actually work against me when it comes to marking. I've decided to take Chris Brown's advice after all and do a PhD through Glasgow (St Andrews) or the Open University. I intend to continue my writing, which includes historical fiction, true-life stories of partying and practical jokes and some comedy sketches. I also develop another little sideline!

Chapter 52
Stuntman

Through the show I did for Channel 4 I was put in touch with a unique specialist agency called Amputees in Action.

The agency was set up by some ex forces amputees and provides amputee 'stunt men' and actors to TV and the movie industry. Their projects include Troy, Band of Brothers, Children of Men and Gladiator, among others. They also supply amputees to NHS and army casualty simulations. This involves the amputee being dressed in an army uniform or civilian clothes and having special make up applied to their arm or leg 'stumps' to make it look as if they have literally just been blown off. The amputee also has a 'part' to play, usually having to memorise various details about the casualty they are playing so as to add realism and so that the medics don't freak out when they see the real thing say in combat. The make up is VERY realistic.

Already the agency has had positive results for the Army, as a recent helicopter crash in Afghanistan saw one soldier become an amputee. The agency received feedback from the medics saying that the experience they gained working with amputee 'stunt men' had helped them save this guy's life and ensured that they hadn't 'freaked out' when they saw him.

I was recently at a training weekend with the agency in York at a RAMC facility and hope to get some work though them soon. All the guys I met there, and Kim who runs the site and the two female makeup artists, were fantastic people and I had a great time. The guys were inspirational to me too and it was handy to swap stories with people who are in a similar position. It's quite ironic that I've ended up with this agency considering my mum was in the RAMC as a territorial and my dad was in the Royal Engineers.

Another project I have in the pipeline is singing for a traditional band that play Scottish and Irish folk songs, though we are at an early stage of planning and I'll know soon what direction we are going to take. One idea I have is becoming a Hibs band, as there doesn't seem to be a proper one at the moment. Hopefully we can be both. I've even penned a few songs, one

Burnt

written to the tune of an Irish song called 'You'll never beat the Irish' but with Hibs lyrics, as follows:

In the 1980s we saw our East Terrace lowered,
The Jambos and their double talk had us fed up and bored,
St Albert scored a brace at Dens to give us all delight
Then Aberdeen exposed the Hearts as mediocre shite

CHORUS
And you'll never beat the Hibees,
No matter what you do
You can put us down and knock us out
But we'll come back again
You know we are the Edinburgh Hibees
And we'll fight until the end
You should have known
You'll never beat the Hibees!

Then in 1990 takeover it was a threat
Fat Wallace and his bankers took advantage of our debt,
They didn't give a damn about
The outrage that they'd cause,
Till hands off Hibs and Sir Tom kicked them squarely in the balls!

(chorus)

T'was less than one year later and the Hibs were on the up,
Keith Wright he scored the semi's goal to put Rangers out the cup,
We won the final against the pars with goals from Tom and Keith,
And the Hibees paraded the trophy down from Princes Street to Leith.

(chorus)

Then 1993 it came, again we had a dream
We took care of UTD, Partick Thistle and Dundee,
The final came and McCoist's winner cut us to the bone
But the Hibees stood defiant and sang 'You'll never walk alone'

(chorus)

Then in 1994 we all had to sit down
They made us go all seater and that made some of us frown
Geebsy's goal it ended Hearts unbeaten derby run
We finished third beat Hearts twice more
Oh what a lot of fun

(chorus)

1996 saw Miller's reign come to an end.
Little did we realise that Duff Jim was round the bend,
He signed lower league diddy men just as if it was for fun
Big Eck came in too late to keep us out of division one

(chorus)

Then in 1999 the Hibees they were back
We won the first division with record points on the rack
The millennium saw us triumph against Jimmy Jeffries men
With Lehmann Sauzee and Miller making the Hibees bounce again!

(chorus)

October 22 in 2000 what a night
We turned it on and showed our class and beat the Jambo shite
A hat trick from big Mixu made the Jambos all feel sick,
Zitelli O'Neil and Russell all scored to make it six!

(chorus)

Less than one year later AEK Athens they came to call
We took them into extra time but that was our downfall
Two goals for the Greeks meant that our hopes weren't very bright
But we were proud when Zitelli won it for us on the night!

(chorus)

Chapter 53
Well?

So that, shall we say, is that. My life in around sixty thousand words. I don't expect anyone to feel sorry for me after reading this, indeed some might not. I wrote this book to try and help other amputees and burns victims, and if I can help even one person by writing it then I will be very happy indeed.

The only ill effects I now suffer other than my disability, which I have grown used to, is periodic bad flashbacks and nightmares. These have affected my relationships with some people since my accident, in that when I was getting them I had a strange desire to be alone, but they are getting less and less frequent all the time, and not as bad.

The only medication I take now is a tablet to stop my grafts from itching at night and the only time I go to hospital is to visit my cool prosthetist Francine, who makes my legs and measures me when I need a new socket if my stump volume has changed. She, like all the medical staff who have cared for me since the fire, has been magnificent and always full of encouragement. I probably owe her a favor for squeezing in emergency repairs on my legs a few times at short notice, but I know she doesn't mind. Like all those who have cared for me, she is highly professional.

In a way, what has happened to me hasn't all been bad, though you may not agree with me after reading this book. My disability has kind of allowed me to opt out of life's rat race and all that 'big house, big car' carry on that people seem to think is so important these days.

I'm upset that no one was jailed over what happened to me and equally upset at not being compensated but I cannot allow that to embitter me, I have far too much to be getting on with now and there is nothing I can do about it anyway, unless there is some kind of miracle.

I think I have adapted superbly to my disability. OK, so I miss playing football and dancing, but it doesn't really stop me from doing anything else, and thankfully it hasn't ruined my social life or my sex life. And I can stand up to pee again.

Burnt

My family have been absolutely amazing throughout the last few years. I love my parents and am glad to be seeing my dad again. My sister has also been amazing, as has my uncle Ron and indeed all of my family. I wish I hadn't caused them all so much heartache and worry though, and I wish my grandparents had lived longer so they could have seen me walking again.

My friends have also been utterly immense. My pals Davie, Martin, Tony, Maggie and John have all been towers of strength to me, as have the new friends I have made along the way. They've never treated me as anything other than a normal guy, though I'm secure enough to know now that I AM still a normal guy, I just have titanium legs and some scars, that's all.

The ironic thing about it all is that my friends say that I am actually generally happier now, which I would for the most part agree with. I certainly don't drink anywhere near as much any more.

As for that football team of mine, Hibs, well, maybe one day we will win the Scottish Cup again but, to be honest, I don't care. I just love going to support them and all the singing and banter that goes with it. Hibs, like my family and friends, were there for me through everything and, like my family and friends, hopefully always will be.

I've no idea what the future holds for me now. I'll just go with the flow for the moment and hopefully keep writing books. I also want to persevere with the acting/stuntman thing, not just for money, but to help create a positive image of the amputee for some people. I'll do that PhD soon as well then I'll maybe look at lecturing in war studies or getting serious history books published. I would even love to help make a decent history of Scotland documentary.

I'm under no illusions about my health. The damage to my kidneys and lungs and my skin grafts may make me susceptible to disease and illness further down the road. I may also require further amputations at some stage in the future but that's all still to come. There is no point in worrying about it, I'm just going to enjoy the rest of my life the best I can. I would love to get married and have kids one day, which is something I would never have considered when I was a drunken waster back in Craigshill. I'm in no rush though, I'd rather wait for Miss Perfect, if she exists.

I mean, look at how Simon Weston, OBE, bounced back from 45 per cent burns when he was serving in the Welsh Fusiliers and on board the Sir Galahad when it was set on fire by enemy bombs in the Falklands War in 1982.

Sometimes in life bad things happen to good people. But what I have learned is that it's not what happens to you or what life throws at you that counts, it's how you react and adapt to it that matters. A phoenix can indeed rise from the flames.

Acknowledgments

I would like to thank my family, my friends, the staff at all the hospitals and rehab centres where I have been treated, Stephen Richards the author and publisher for giving me a chance, Olivia, Joe McGuire, Rachel Curran, Amputees in Action, Duncan, everyone from Craigshill, St Andrews RC in Livingston, the 'bounce' (you know who you are) and its kind administrators for letting me run amok, Lynn Nelson, Chris Brown, Stuart McHardy, Caroline Anderson, Loura Brooks, Mixu Paatelainen and Hibernian FC, Lothian and Borders police and Aidan Lyons for all their help, support, encouragement and downright heroism at various stages of my recovery.

Special Mention

Brook, Lapping Productions for the film 'Blood in the Water', now renamed 'Ocean Of Fear'.
Director - Richard Bedser
Line producer - Charlotte Wheaton
Photography director - Malcolm MacLean
Drama scenes shot at Pinewood Studios, Bucks, England. Other scenes at HMS Belfast and Nassau, Bahamas.

Some Other Titles From Mirage Publishing

Cosmic Ordering Guide
- Stephen Richards
Cosmic Ordering Connection
- Stephen Richards
Cosmic Ordering Service: 101 Orders For Daily Use
- Stephen Richards
Cosmic Ordering: Oracle Wish Cards
- Stephen Richards & Karen Whitelaw Smith
The Butterfly Experience: Inspiration For Change
- Karen Whitelaw Smith

Prospective titles

Past Life Tourism
- Barbara Ford-Hammond
Cosmic Ordering: Oracle Healing Cards
- Stephen Richards
The Tumbler: Kassa (Košice) - Auschwitz - Sweden - Israel
- Azriel Feuerstein
Occult: Dispatches From The Shadows
- Jonathan Charles Tapsell
The Butterfly Experience: Transformation Oracle Cards
- Karen Whitelaw Smith
The Butterfly Experience - Transforming Lives (Self Relaxation CD)
- Karen Whitelaw Smith
The Real Office: An Uncharacteristic Gesture of Magnanimity
by Management Supremo Hilary Wilson-Savage
- Hilary Wilson-Savage
Rebel Diet: They Don't Want You To Have It!
- Emma James

Mirage Publishing Website:
www.miragepublishing.com

Submissions of Mind, Body & Spirit manuscripts
welcomed from new authors.